THE Q/OMNIBUS PRESS ROCK'N'ROLL READER

Given away free with Q91, April 1994

"Rock journalism is people who can't write,
preparing stories based on interviews
with people who can't talk, in order to
amuse people who can't read."

Frank Zappa

Let's not get carried away, Frank. More rubbish *has*
been written about rock than about almost any other
institution or art form in history. Equally, though,
popular music has inspired some beautiful
journalism, criticism and language. Plenty of it
appears in Q (we hope) and in books published by
Omnibus Press (we know). It was a short mental hop,
then, to the pooling of resources that ultimately led to
the gorgeous tome you presently hold. The fact that
we've managed to get the whole thing to you free of
charge is probably just more proof that there *is* a
God. Some of the pieces gathered in this book are
sad; others are funny, informative, bewildering,
revelatory, inspiring or just plain weird. All are
evidence for the defence against m'learned friend
Mr Zappa's accusations. You be the judge.
Prepare for deep enjoyment.

Danny Kelly (Editor, Q)

THE Q/OMNIBUS PRESS ROCK'N'ROLL READER

Presented free with Q91, March 1994

Edited by Danny Kelly

Concept: Katherine Allen, Hilary Donlon

Compiled by: John Aizlewood, David Cavanagh, Andrew Collins,
Adrian Deevoy, Danny Kelly

Production: John Bauldie, Mark Pickard

Typesetting: The Type Bureau

Printed and bound in Great Britain by
Cox & Wyman Ltd, Reading, Berkshire

Cover photo: Dennis Morris from Never Mind The B*ll*cks – A Photographic
Record Of The Sex Pistols (Omnibus Press)

Invaluable assistance: Sue Hawken, Bill Prince, Maria De Rosa, Phil Webb,
Jerry Perkins, Tim Harrison, Andy Cowles, Andrew King, Brian McAughey,
Richard Carman, Sam Gathercole, Audrey Sampson, Selwyn Garner,
Kimberly Kriete, Pamela Craddock, Pearce Marchbank, Colour Systems Ltd

CONTENTS

ELVIS

The Final Years

JERRY HOPKINS

**Elvis Presley is history's most written-about
entertainer. And within that torrent of paper and ink,
he's simultaneously the most adored and vilified
artist of all time. From the dewy-eyed devotion of
countless fan-aimed publications to the surgically
applied vitriol of Albert Goldman, you can have your
Elvis however you want. Hopkins's book, thankfully,
avoids such extremes and concentrates on The
King's horrific yet strangely entertaining last seven
years. Its opening chapter, reproduced here, lowers
the reader straight into the industrial-strength
weirdness in which Presley so often found himself
adrift. It's Winter, 1970; Elvis is a megastar with
unusual dietary requirements; Richard Nixon is in the
White House, organising the illegal destruction of
Laos and Cambodia . . .**

IT MAY HAVE been the most unusual weekend in Elvis Presley's
life, although it was so typical, too. It began in Memphis on
Saturday, December 19, 1970, with a fiery family fight. It was
Elvis's father Vernon's job to write the personal checks and
when he came at Elvis with a handful of bills, shaking his head
the way he always did, Elvis mumbled, "Fuck . . . here we go
again."

"Elvis," Vernon began, "somethin' here we gotta talk about."

"Yeah . . ."

"Lookit, Elvis, I know you don't like me sayin' anythin' about your money, but I just got these in from California and I wanna check 'em with you. There must be a mistake, because this one's from Kerr's and it says you charged $38,000 in guns there this month."

"Christmas shoppin', daddy. That's all."

Vernon merely shook his head and shuffled the bits of paper around. He knew the next one probably was accurate, too. "This other's from the Mercedes place in Hollywood. Says you bought six cars there last week for eighty thousand . . ."

"Those are the big presents, daddy. One's for 'Cilla, 'nother's for Sheriff Morris . . ."

"Now, Elvis, how many times I got to say it? Vegas pays you real good and the Colonel says now you're tourin' again, there's gonna be good money there, too, but we just not makin' that kinda money these days to spend so much as this and . . ."

Elvis had heard it all before. His daddy had grown up poor in Mississippi, a sharecropper and sometime ditchdigger who went to jail for forging a check to buy groceries. That was during the Great Depression, when Elvis was three years old. Only the Internal Revenue Service had bothered to count the millions of dollars that Elvis had earned in the years since.

By the time Elvis appeared on The Ed Sullivan Show, from the waist up, in 1956, soon after Heartbreak Hotel was released, the lines were drawn: Elvis was adjudged a threat, by parents and teachers and ministers, and by this declaration the generation gap was defined. Elvis's daddy and the parents of all his followers came from a security-conscious generation, veterans of that terrible Depression, while Elvis's, coming out of the 1950s, was freedom-seeking and believed in testing authority.

For many, then, Elvis was the original Fonz, the archetypal greaser or rocker who became a model for a rebellious age. "They all think I'm a sex maniac," he told an interviewer at the time, speaking of his critics. "They're just frustrated old types anyway. I'm just natural."

Yet, Elvis was not a rebel, not really. He enjoyed the role, it was clear, but it was also apparent that he hated it. He was genuinely hurt by the criticism he got in the '50s. It embarrassed him in front of his doting mother, who'd taught him to call everyone "sir" and "ma'am," a habit he maintained until his death.

It wasn't surprising, then, when Elvis became a rather bland figure, a patriot willing to gamble his career to serve two years in the army, a loving son who wept openly at his mother's death, a performer who returned to civilian life a crooner of ballads and opera (It's Now Or Never). He sought approval in established areas, becoming an innocuous actor who ambled good-naturedly through dozens of sappy but wholesome Hollywood musicals, and then went where only the most established stars performed, Las Vegas.

Never was there any rough edge, a drunken fight, an arrest, a sex scandal, such as was the case in the careers of Sinatra and Brando and most of the younger rock stars of the 1960s. He didn't say he was bigger than Jesus, as Beatle John Lennon did; Elvis worshipped Him, openly, and recorded albums of gospel songs. He also took an apolitical stance, refusing to reveal his conservative beliefs for fear of offending. He generously supported dozens of charities and hundreds of needy individuals.

Thus, Elvis became two-dimensional, inoffensive, a slate upon which nearly everyone could scratch his or her fantasy. And it was a slate you could wipe clean afterward, changing your fantasy at any time, without fear that Elvis would do anything to make that dangerous.

In the 1950s, Elvis seemed to be rebelling against the establishment. In the 1960s – the Hollywood years – he was embraced by the establishment. And as the 1970s began, he *was*

7

the establishment. A lot of people could identify with that kind of success. But not his daddy.

Elvis glared at his father and finally said, "Daddy, it's only money. There's more where it came from . . ."

"But, son . . ."

Elvis gritted his teeth and growled, "Daddy, I don't want to talk about it!"

Usually Elvis tried to keep his temper in check, but tonight Priscilla joined Vernon; she hated his wild spending, too. When Elvis wanted, he could be the model of Christian patience. His fury also was legendary. When the gates to his Graceland estate weren't opened promptly enough by his gatekeepers – most of whom were relatives – he was famous for ordering the limousine driven *through* the gates. How many times had he angrily humiliated the guys who worked for him? How many television sets had he shot out with his derringer? There were many things that aroused his ire and being told what to do was one of them.

"Lookit, goddammit," he said, "it's my fuckin' money and I can do whatever in goddamn hell I want with it!"

When the shouting had stopped and a taut silence had constricted the room, Elvis aloofly stalked out of the mansion, wearing a purple velvet suit and cape, gold belt buckle, amber glasses, carrying a jewelled white cane and a .45 calibre pistol in a shoulder holster. He then drove one of his cars to Memphis International Airport and for the first time in his life, he bought a ticket on a commercial airliner and flew to another city, *alone.*

Elvis had never done anything like this before. Why, at the age of 35 he'd never even been in a bank. (No need to: When he was young, he was poor; when he was older he had people to take care of such things.) Surrounded by salaried lackeys for nearly 15 years – even through his army duty in Germany – he was effectively isolated from ordinary life and society. And now he was on his way to Washington, boarding not a chartered jet but a commercial airliner to sit with Real People.

His destination wasn't selected randomly, or in anger. There was purpose and determination in making this flight and Elvis had planned it for some time, although only John O'Grady knew about it. O'Grady was a tough ex-narcotics cop, now a private detective who had been hired a year or so earlier by Elvis's attorney, for help in a paternity suit. Sometime after that, O'Grady says, he started Elvis collecting police badges.

"I was a cop for 20 years, a sergeant in charge of the Hollywood narcotics detail. I knew when people were doped up and Elvis was strung out on pills. Now, I'm not saying he didn't have prescriptions for those pills, but he was strung out. If you know what to look for, the eyes, the slurred or speeded-up speech, I mean, 20 years and I *knew*, so I figured if he started carrying badges around, maybe he'd stop taking that shit. I was in Hawaii talking about industrial security at a cops' convention in 1969 and I met John Finlator, the deputy US narcotics director. Elvis said he wanted a US narcotics badge to add to his collection. I set up a meeting. I thought it might help."

Of course, Elvis had his own reasons for meeting the nation's number two narc. He carried a pistol almost everywhere he went these days – sometimes even to bed, stuck into the waistband of his custom-made silk pyjamas or in the pocket of his robe. He and some of his boys had deputy sheriffs' badges and permits to carry sidearms in Memphis, courtesy of his friend Sheriff Bill Morris, and in Palm Springs, where he owned another house. Elvis believed that if he had a federal badge it would allow him to go armed everywhere in the United States.

There was another reason he wanted the badge. For Elvis, the word "drugs" meant heroin, and he often talked with his friends about how that, along with Communism and

Communist sympathizers like Jane Fonda and Rap Brown, constituted one of the country's most insidious threats. "He talked with other performers in Vegas," says Jerry Schilling, one of Elvis's closest friends the last 11 years. "They were junkies and after he talked to them, they stopped taking drugs. I know that sounds far out, but it's true. I personally know of two individuals who stopped taking heroin. Elvis figured if he had a federal narcotics badge, he could maybe scare some other entertainers into kicking dope."

Elvis reported to the American Airlines check-in counter in Memphis, where he was sold a ticket and whisked into the VIP lounge and then boarded on the flight to the capital separately. Thus he didn't go through the security check for weapons and his pistol wasn't discovered. He also was travelling under the name John Burroughs, a name he'd used for years for personal mail and telephone calls. In Washington, he hailed a taxi to the Washington Hotel. What happened on the way was one of the stories Elvis would tell and retell about the weekend. "He had the driver stop at one of those ghetto donut joints on the way to the hotel," says T.G. Sheppard, another friend. "He had his diamonds on his fingers and he had his gun and one of the people there says, 'Allll-visss Presley – lookit them diamond rings on you hands, man, Lord have mercy!' And Elvis says, 'Yeah, man, an' I'm gone keep 'em too'; and he pulls the .45 outta the shoulder holster. He'd laugh when he tol' this story. He had the deepest laugh I ever heard. He laughed all the way down to his soul."

Once at the hotel, Elvis made a number of calls to Los Angeles, as well as plans to go there. Why is not clear. His meeting with Finlator was set for Monday morning and he may simply have become lonely, and so flew to California because it was the place where he knew he had friends, outside of Memphis. Or he may have been caught up in the James Bond-ish nature of the whole thing and this was the way he

10

played it. Elvis loved spy movies and Clint Eastwood was one of his favourite movie stars; he enjoyed bringing such drama into his own life any way he could. His erratic behaviour also could be explained by illness or drugs.

First he called Gerald Peters, a 50-ish Englishman who'd recently begun chauffeuring Elvis around in Los Angeles. When the operator told him "Mr. Burroughs" was calling, and there was no response, Elvis broke in and whispered, "Sir Gerald . . . it's me . . ."

Elvis told Gerald he was in Washington and said he was coming to Los Angeles. Twenty minutes later he called to say he'd changed his mind and 30 minutes after that he called another time to say he was arriving on Trans World Airways flight number 85, arriving at 1.17am. He swore Gerald to absolute secrecy regarding his present whereabouts and plans and then called Jerry Schilling.

Jerry was a big, good-looking former football player for Arkansas State University who'd worked for Elvis off and on for about five years, first as a movie stand-in and then as a personal bodyguard. Following Elvis's instructions he called Gerald and together, in secrecy in the middle of the night, they drove to the airport to meet The Boss.

The picture Jerry paints is executed in a mix of bold and subtle strokes. One-thirty in the morning and there's Elvis exiting the plane still wearing his cape and purple velvet suit, a stewardess on each arm. Jerry also notices that Elvis's face is swollen up . . . and then he sees that Elvis is carrying, besides the cane, a small cardboard box. Jerry looked into it and counted a toothbrush, small complimentary-size toothpaste and soap, a little washrag.

"What's that?"

"Well," he said innocently, "I had to get some stuff for travelling."

Elvis had Jerry call a doctor to meet them at his home and

then, on the way in from the airport, they took the girls home. It was then that Elvis told Jerry the story about what had happened in Washington when he told the airline ticket agent he was boarding with a pistol. The agent followed him on to the plane.

"I'm sorry, Mr. Presley, but you cannot fly on this plane with a gun."

Elvis angrily left the plane, fairly running down the staircase. The pilot, who was watching, followed him and ran along behind on the tarmac, calling, "Mr. Presley, please come back! This is the pilot, please accept our apology . . ."

Elvis finished telling the story as they rode up the drive of his sumptuous estate in a rich section called Holmby Hills. The doctor was waiting at the gate. Elvis told Jerry his swollen face was a reaction to a penicillin shot. It's not clear if this is true; when and under what circumstances did Elvis get such medication? Was it reaction to one of the prescribed drugs he took regularly? Years later, his physician would say Elvis frequently suffered severe allergic reaction to several drugs. Whatever the cause of the problem, the doctor in attendance this night in California gave Elvis a shot of his own and Elvis slept for eight hours.

At noon Sunday when he woke up, Elvis hollered for Jerry and when Jerry came running, he said, "I want you to come to Washington with me." He didn't tell Jerry why.

"Aw, Elvis, look, I just took this job at Paramount and if I go to Washington tonight I'll miss work tomorrow, this is important to me . . ."

"Don't worry about it. I'll charter you a jet."

"Elvis, there's no way I can make it there physically and get back to work in time."

Elvis looked down at his feet, a little boy toeing the ground, and said, "OK, I'll go by myself."

Jerry sighed resignedly and began making arrangements for

12

the trip. He called the Washington Hotel and reserved two rooms – yes, they remembered "John Burroughs" – and then booked two seats on a flight leaving about 10 o'clock that night. Now Elvis was travelling under another alias, Dr. John Carpenter, the name of the character he'd portrayed only a year earlier in a film called Change Of Habit. On the way to the airport, Gerald stopped at the Beverly Hills Hotel so Elvis could cash a check for $500. Jerry and Elvis had had no cash between them and Jerry assured Elvis that "you can charge plane tickets and hotel rooms and meals to credit cards, but you really can't travel properly unless you got money for tips and incidentals." Elvis looked at him as if he didn't know what he was talking about, but nodded his approval.

By now, Elvis had been gone from Memphis for more than 24 hours and his family and friends were frantic. At first they thought he'd merely gone for a ride to cool off following the fight. Then they began to make casual inquiries. Joe Esposito and Charlie Hodge, two of Elvis's hired hands, both started calling around the country. Gerald was one of many who got calls: "Uh, by the way, you haven't heard from Elvis, have you?" Gerald of course said no.

When Elvis boarded the plane in Los Angeles, every seat was full. Christmas was only five days away and in 1970 that meant every plane heading East from California was carrying soldiers on leave from Vietnam. About half the passengers on the flight were in uniform. Elvis, seated on the aisle, struck up a conversation with several of the men. It was late, but the mood was up, people were in the aisles laughing and talking.

"Elvis and I settled down," Jerry says, "and pretty soon he tells me he's going to write a letter. Now, I think Elvis in his whole life only wrote three or four letters. He tells me he's going to Washington to get a federal narcotics badge from John Finlator and he is writing a letter to the President of the United States, President Nixon. He asked me to proofread the letter."

In the letter Elvis expressed freely his ideas about Jane Fonda and Communism and especially drugs, showing concern about the role popular musicians and singers played in this. He said he wanted to do something positive and wanted to talk to Nixon about that. He told the President he was staying at the Washington Hotel under the name John Burroughs, gave his room number, and suggested he call his personal public relations man, Jerry Schilling, to make an appointment.

"Well, first of all," Jerry says, "there was a lot of grammar and stuff that probably could've been changed. But I knew where his heart was in the letter and I liked it the way he wrote it, so I said, 'Elvis, it's perfect the way it is.'"

Jerry returned to his book after reading the letter, and Elvis started talking to another GI. After a few minutes, he poked Jerry in the ribs. "Jerry," he said, "where's the money?"

"I got it, it's safe . . . why?"

"Jerry, give it to me."

Both men were whispering. Jerry said, "Elvis, this is our expense money. You can't . . ."

Elvis said, "Jerry, this soldier's going home for Christmas and I want to make it a good one for him and his loved ones."

"Elvis, we won't have any money for tips and . . ."

Elvis gritted his teeth and said, "The guy . . . just . . . got . . . back . . . from . . . Vietnam." So Jerry gave him the $500 and Elvis gave it to the soldier and said, "Merry Christmas."

The plane arrived in the capital Monday, December 21, at 6.30am. Elvis had eaten a half-box of candy that someone had given him and again his face was swollen. Jerry saw Elvis to the waiting limousine and called the hotel, telling the desk to get a doctor. Elvis said he wanted to go to the White House first.

"Elvis, it's 6.30 in the morning. Let's check with the doctor first and clean up . . ."

"Godammit, Jerry, we're going to the White House *now*!"

They rode silently to 1600 Pennsylvania Avenue as Elvis took out his pen and covered a portion of the envelope containing his letter: "Personal – For the President's Eyes Only." Driving to the guard gate, Elvis got out of the car and, extending his hand with the envelope, he said, "Sir . . .?" The guard looked right through him, as if Elvis didn't exist.

Elvis glanced back at Jerry as if he didn't know what to do, as if his feelings were hurt at not being recognized. Then he remembered his mussed clothing, shoulder-length hair, and tinted glasses.

"Oh," he said to the guard, "uh, uh, I'm Elvis Presley and I have a letter for the President and . . ."

The guard snapped to and smiled broadly, apologizing, and when Elvis explained his mission, he said he'd see the letter was delivered as soon as Nixon was in his office. The limousine then took Elvis to the hotel.

After the doctor left, Jerry asked if he could call Memphis. "Elvis," he said, "you've been gone for two days and I'm very worried about your father and Priscilla. They must be going crazy. I gave you my word and you know me, I'm not going to break it. But can I call down there and say you're with me and you're OK? We don't have to say where you are . . . and I've got to get back to my job, so I'd like to have Sonny come up here." Sonny West was another of Elvis's full-time bodyguards.

Elvis agreed and told Jerry to stay at the hotel to take the President's call. He then left the hotel alone to take the limousine to John Finlator's office, leaving Finlator's number with Jerry.

Finlator was expecting "Mr. Burroughs" and, leaving a wake of startled secretaries and intermediaries behind him, Elvis was ushered quickly into the deputy director's office. Elvis got right down to business. He said he wanted to donate $5,000 to Finlator's department. Finlator was startled by the offer, graciously refusing it, explaining that his department was funded by the taxpayers, so Elvis already was a contributor.

At first Elvis thought Finlator was reacting the way others did when he suddenly gave them expensive rings and cars. So he did what he usually did. He laughed and said, "It's OK . . . really . . . I want to do it." Elvis knew from experience that most people refused a magnanimous gesture at first, but always accepted eventually.

John Finlator wasn't like the others and he said no again. Elvis wasn't certain how to handle this rejection, so he told the deputy director how he'd already talked two entertainers into getting off heroin in Las Vegas.

"And, uh, uh . . . if I had a badge from your department, sir, I'm sure I could do more good work. Sir, that's why I'd like you to give me a badge."

Finlator said he'd be pleased to arrange for an honorary badge.

"Uh, no sir, that is, it's important to me to have the real thing."

So saying, Elvis then produced his deputy's badges from Memphis and Palm Springs.

Again Finlator was struck dumb and again he turned Elvis down. It was impossible, he said. There were regulations. It was not a choice. It was out of his hands.

"Elvis was depressed when I got him on the phone in Finlator's office," Jerry Schilling says, "and before I could say anything he said, 'Jerry, I can't do any good here, I'm coming back to the hotel.' I interrupted him. I said, 'Why I'm calling, Elvis, is the President wants to see you right away.'"

Amazingly, the letter had reached Nixon and he cleared 20 minutes in his schedule. Elvis told Jerry he'd pick him up in the limo and before leaving asked Finlator one more question.

"You won't mind if I ask the President for the badge, will you, sir?"

Finlator chuckled and said no, go ahead, because that was the only way the department could give him one.

When Elvis returned to the hotel he found Jerry waiting and Sonny checking in. Together they went to the White House, where they were met by Egil "Bud" Krogh, Nixon's top enforcement officer, later convicted as one of the Watergate conspirators. When they told him they were armed, he advised them to leave their pistols in the car. Except for one. This was a gold-plated commemorative World War II Colt .45 that Elvis had picked up while in Los Angeles as a gift for the President. This was given to Krogh, who checked to see that it was empty, whereupon Elvis finally was sent into the Oval Office.

Jerry and Sonny were disappointed when Elvis left them behind. Krogh explained that it required more security if more than one person went in.

"Well," Sonny said, "I know Elvis and he'll ask the President to let us in."

At that moment the inter-office telephone buzzed. It was the President, asking that Jerry and Sonny be allowed in. At the same time, Elvis appeared at the door and said, "Come on in, guys, I want you to meet the President."

Elvis was grinning broadly, as excited as a small boy. As soon as Elvis met Nixon he explained his need for the federal badge and Nixon told Krogh to take care of it.

Jerry and Sonny hesitated at the door to the President's office, clearly nervous about entering. Elvis laughed and said, "C'mon, c'mon . . ." For years afterward he would retell the story of this meeting and always tease his bodyguards about their timidity.

Nixon came forward and shook their hands stiffly. "Elvis, you got a couple of pretty big guys here. It looks like Elvis is in pretty good hands with you two. You guys play football?"

The small talk continued for a few minutes as the White House photographer snapped several pictures, one formal shot of Elvis and Nixon, other more candid shots around the President's desk. Then Elvis said, "Mr. President . . . you know that Presidential button you gave me?"

Nixon started and said, "Oh yes . . ." and pulled two more lapel pins from a drawer, coming around the desk to hand them to Jerry and Sonny.

"Uh . . . sir . . ." Elvis said. "They've got wives, sir."

The President started again, returning hurriedly to his desk to get two brooches. Nixon then walked the trio to the door, patted Elvis awkwardly on the shoulder and told Krogh to take the boys on a tour of the house. The badge arrived 20 minutes later.

It was a weekend of such exquisite paradox – only three days, a drop in life's bucket, yet a Saturday-through-Monday gem nonetheless, one which revealed much about Elvis and his world. Western civilization was full of boys who never grew up, especially in the United States. Elvis was one of these, a full-sized grown-up who had a fight with his father and reacted by running away from home. And what did he do next? He played cops and robbers in Washington. Flying alone for the first time, indulgently eating a half-pound of chocolates, refusing to take no for an answer from authority figures (the Washington ticket agent, John Finlator), writing the President of the United States and expecting a meeting to result, believing that whatever you wanted you got, openly sharing his possessions (guns and money) – in almost every move he made, Elvis showed himself to be an eternal child, trapped in a cocoon of his own spinning, innocent, naive, protected, and more than a little spoiled.

In the afternoon, Jerry returned to Los Angeles, to report to work at Paramount the following day without explanation (who'd have believed him?), and Elvis and Sonny went back to Memphis, where Elvis strode into Graceland and shouted to Priscilla, "Hi, hon, I'm home."

MORRISSEY AND MARR: THE SEVERED ALLIANCE

The Definitive Story Of The Smiths

JOHNNY ROGAN

When Johnny Rogan's exhaustive history of the '80s best-loved band was first published, Morrissey responded by saying he hoped the author would die in a motorway pile-up. Despite this, the book has become recognised as a classic. In this extract the band, no longer the inseparable gang they once were, try to complete their masterwork, The Queen Is Dead . . .

THE SMITHS OPENED 1986 in a position of stalemate. Unable to record new material, they were doubly frustrated by the postponement of their new album, which Rough Trade was keeping on ice until the legal dispute was settled. Johnny Marr went through an uncharacteristically dark period at this point, as if realizing that the group's future was in severe jeopardy. He had worked extremely hard producing the album and felt exhilarated prior to its completion. "Johnny was so sick of it that he asked me, 'Could you finish it off?'" John Porter recalled. The producer duly engineered Frankly Mr Shankly at the close of the sessions. "The album did him in," Porter revealed. "It was a lot of responsibility."

Marr's life might have been easier had he been allowed to concentrate solely on the music and production. All too often, however, he was plagued by the inevitable legacy of The

Smiths' continued lack of management: wearying business and legal wrangles. At a crucial point during the sessions, a representative from Rough Trade telephoned the studio with the disturbing news that The Smiths' van hire company was pressing charges because the group had neglected to return a truck. It was at this point that Marr realized he was taking on too much. At earlier times, he had been known to socialize and party after a session, but The Queen Is Dead involved intense evenings working on overdubs and planning the following day's recordings. "Johnny became insular and detached from myself and Andy," Joyce recalls. "He was taking on a lot and wanted to do it himself. I remember him not wanting us around for awhile."

The isolation evidently took its toll. "It was really tough," Marr confirms. "I locked myself away for a couple of weeks after I finished that record. I sat in a chair, didn't move and got depressed, which was pretty unlike me. I lost loads of weight and was very skinny and unhealthy. I was ill quite a lot in The Smiths, being a hyper person. I've calmed down quite a lot. I used to throw up all the time. The Queen Is Dead was very difficult."

In the creative vacuum that followed the album, Marr and Rourke joined Billy Bragg on the Red Wedge tour. The full Smiths line-up played a four-song set at Newcastle City Hall, but their singer seemed bemused by it all. "I didn't really understand what was going on on stage," he recalls. "It all seemed a little limp to me, even though there were people involved that I do admire."

The following week, the group joined New Order and The Fall for "From Manchester With Love", a benefit concert in aid of 49 Liverpool councillors who were being taken to court by the government for refusing to set a legal rate. Predictably, Morrissey/Marr were absent from the preliminary meeting between councillor Derek Hatton, Mark E. Smith and New Order. It was left to Stuart James to act as The Smiths' shoulder-shrugging representative. The concert at Liverpool's Royal Court was reasonably successful, but merely proved a deceptive prelude to what was arguably the biggest crisis in the group's career.

The "Irish tour" was, by now, a traditional part of The Smiths' gigging calendar and provided some of their most relaxed and convivial moments. The trip across the water coincided with the usual drinking session but, for Andy Rourke, stronger substances were required. The following evening at the National Stadium, Dublin, the group's set was marred by a lacklustre display from the troubled bassist. Given Rourke's integral importance to The Smiths' live performance, it was difficult to disguise his shortcomings. As Grant Showbiz remarked: "Andy had lost it. Out of 10 notes, he was playing three. He was completely gone and just stopped playing numbers . . . Everybody was deeply concerned about Andy."

Although the other two dates, at Dundalk's Fairways Hotel and Queen's University, Belfast, passed without incident, the state of Rourke became a biting issue. Precisely a year before, he had been warned of the need to stay straight while working with The Smiths, and this public relapse had broken that pact. "It was difficult with Andy because he was out of it all the time and it got to the point where you had to take a stance," Joyce remarked. "It not only affected his playing but when we were together. It was difficult to get through to him." Although the drummer had broached the subject with Rourke, the bassist knew that his partner had no experience of addiction. "You don't understand" was Andy's weary response whenever advice was dished out.

Marr was uncertain about what action to take against his friend, feeling that it was almost hypocritical to adopt a self-righteous attitude. "They had this friendship that was so strong that it was tearing Johnny to pieces," Grant explained. "I was one of the people who said we should get rid of Andy. I felt it would be for the best. The only way for him to sort himself out was to be kicked out of the band and told that he would have to stop taking drugs." On stage with Rourke, Marr had realized the extent of his partner's troubles. "He just wasn't in a state to play," he observed. "That was the thing. It

21

was more so when he was trying to come off heroin, and that's what happened on that Irish tour. He finally took too much methadone and wasn't fun to be around."

Morrissey and Marr informed Rourke of their decision and he accepted the news stoically. Far from arguing his case, he realized that he was in danger of letting the group down, which only made the dismissal more difficult. "It was really painful, but it had been on the cards for some time," Johnny recalls. "That was one of the low points of my life. Seeing Andy taking a couple of his basses from my house and getting in his car was really upsetting. But I knew he'd get over it."

After returning from Ireland, Marr urgently sought a replacement bassist. Drummer Simon Wolstencroft suggested Craig Gannon, whom he had played alongside in The Colourfield. Gannon was a talented journeyman guitarist, whose curriculum vitae included stints with Aztec Camera and The Bluebells. Marr initially offered Gannon the bassist spot, secure in the knowledge that, should Andy return, the new arrival could be retained as a second guitarist. Events took an unhappy turn the following week when Rourke was arrested for possession of heroin. On a purely expedient note, this might have prompted a complete ostracism, but instead, his friends rallied around. "We were convinced that if we let him go, we'd find he was dead in six months," Grant confessed. "I was convinced of that and I think Johnny was too. The only thing that was seemingly holding Andy together was The Smiths. We were proved wrong, though, as you so often are with these things."

The double shock of being fired from The Smiths and arrested convinced Rourke that his heroin habit had to be banished permanently. Those who suspected that Morrissey's anti-drug stance would harden the singer against Rourke underestimated his humanity. "His leaving seemed more wrong than his staying," the vocalist confirmed. "It was too easy to turn like a pack and say, 'You're useless. Get out.'" As a result, the group reconsidered their decision and invited the errant bassist to return. On this occasion, he kept his promise and stayed straight. "When he left, he became even more depressed than when he was with the group," Morrissey recalls. "It was getting quite serious so he really had to come back . . . It seemed very unnatural and ridiculous to even consider such things as session musicians and people from other parts of the country." To Rourke's credit, he never fell out with his fellow Smiths, despite his bouts of drug dependence. "I've never come across a junkie who wasn't a bastard, except Andy," Johnny reasoned. "He never turned into a bastard in his life, and that's the first thing that usually happens. He came out of it and he's still not bitter, unbalanced or nasty, and he never was. The only person he ever took it out on was himself. There was great moral courage there, against the odds."

The rehabilitation of Rourke stabilized The Smiths at a time when they were under immense legal, creative and personal pressures. A further twist was added to the story when Craig Gannon was kept on as additional guitarist following Rourke's return. Marr realized that Gannon's adaptability would be beneficial to The Smiths in various ways. Johnny already had the considerable burden of approximating live the multi-track, wall-of-sound, guitar displays concocted in the studio, and this process would prove more challenging than ever with the release of their new album. It was intended that Gannon should beef up The Smiths' sound and prevent Marr from spreading himself too thinly. The restructuring of The Smiths also encouraged Johnny to explore new ideas and, over the next year, his influence on the musical direction of the group would be more profound than ever.

In the aftermath of the Rourke affair, The Smiths continued their renegotiation with Rough Trade. Marr had already introduced a buccaneering element to the proceedings by commandeering roadie Phil Powell in an attempt to liberate the master tapes by cloak and dagger methods. One snowy evening, they set off from Manchester and drove to Guildford, intent on bluffing their way into the studios. The plan was foiled. With Travis maintaining his ground, the group found a more orthodox solution to their woes by re-enlisting Matthew Sztumpf as their manager. Working in tandem with solicitors, Sztumpf entered delicate negotiations with Travis. Neither party welcomed the prospect of proceedings to trial since, apart from the intimidating legal fees, the release of the lucrative new album could be postponed for a further year. Travis held firm, but agreed to increase Morrissey/Marr's advance and, more importantly, reduced their outstanding contractual commitment from two albums to one (excluding compilations and live recordings). The essential profit-sharing system remained intact and no attempt was made to append the names of the other Smiths to the revised agreement.

Within weeks of the renegotiation, Morrissey and Marr were discussing where they might record their next studio album. They planned to move to America, complete some sessions and concentrate on touring. In retrospect, it seems remarkable that the "travel-shy" Morrissey would countenance such a radical proposal but, for a time, he seemed taken with the idea. Accompanied by Sztumpf, the duo flew to Los Angeles and looked at a number of apartments, but none proved suitable. After promising to continue the search later in the year, they returned to the UK and promptly forgot all about the grand scheme. Their flightiness descended upon the perplexed Sztumpf, who soon discovered that his services were no longer required. "My mistake was not saying, 'I won't lift a finger until contracts are signed between us'," he reflects. "But that's not the way I work. The injunction had to be sorted out immediately . . . I wasn't there long enough for royalties to be commissioned, so I just billed them for my services. I'd fulfilled my purpose, but they paid me, and I enjoyed it while it lasted." Ironically, Sztumpf was in the process of setting up a European tour when the axe fell. Not surprisingly, the Continental jaunt was swiftly abandoned.

The convenient dismissal of Sztumpf reiterated The Smiths' determination to maintain control of their financial and artistic destinies; it also underlined a fundamental naïvety about the function of management. Marr gave the mistaken impression that he regarded Sztumpf as a potential hatchet man of Allen Klein proportions. In a discussion with Grant Showbiz, Johnny portrayed Sztumpf as the new broom who would prefer to bring in his own men and might even rid The Smiths of several key personnel. In fact, it was Sztumpf himself who felt pressurized into making changes. At one point, Morrissey cheekily suggested that he should forego managing Madness and concentrate entirely on The Smiths. Eventually, Sztumpf compromised by moving his office to a "neutral ground" away from the heart of the Madness empire. "The Smiths were always concerned that Madness would come first and I'd be playing second fiddle," he complained.

Morrissey's conviction that another act would distract Sztumpf from a total commitment to The Smiths betrayed a myopic perspective of the pop management role. With Madness and The Smiths on his roster, Sztumpf's clout and standing in the industry would have improved vastly and enabled him to negotiate from a stronger position. What Morrissey required was the subservient "neutered lackey" manager, a species that is not only entirely dependent on the artiste, but commands little respect from more powerful business rivals. Morrissey's possessive personality consistently prevented him from allowing anybody to "manage" The Smiths. After abandoning Sztumpf, he again fell back on non-managerial employees, who were nevertheless called upon to perform quasi-managerial tasks. Martha Defoe, an excellent organizer who had already proven her worth during the formation of Smithdom, fell in and out of favour, but lacked the music business experience to assume the traditional managerial role. As Scott Piering noted: "Martha wasn't a Jazz Summers who could really go in and kick ass with CBS, but she was someone they could trust." Defoe's strength was her directness and determined efficiency. She claims Morrissey once gave her the ultimate passing compliment: "Whatever you say you'll do, I'm always sure it will happen." Although sensitive to the personal dynamics within the group, Defoe remained closest to Morrissey, which may have proven a fault as well as a virtue. "Martha, in the end, figuratively fell in love with Morrissey and was totally besotted with him," Piering observed. "As soon as you start getting that way with Morrissey, your days are numbered. Many times, when things were fine, Morrissey was just keeping Martha at bay. Alternatively, he loved the attention he got from her. Intellectually, they were equals; she could relate to him, knew what books to buy him, and she was very good for Morrissey. But she clung to him."

Morrissey's love of feminine solicitude was emphasized by the number of women whom he relied upon as administrators. In addition to his mother and Martha Defoe, there was Pat Bellis, whose tasks stretched far beyond those of the normal record company press officer. Jo Slee, who enjoyed a separate sleeve artwork agreement with Morrissey, was another confidante who could always be relied upon to provide help whenever asked. Morrissey's band of female supporters was of considerable assistance during The Smiths' lengthy periods of self-management, but ultimately proved an inadequate substitute for a full-time, experienced, personal/business manager.

The upheavals of early 1986 were placed in a more pleasing perspective with the release of the long-awaited new Smiths single in May. The initial airing on BBC Radio One's Janice Long evening show was a devastatingly dramatic moment and I still recall standing in my ascetically sparse, under-equipped kitchen, frozen in gleeful awe. Bigmouth Strikes Again was a superbly structured single, which revealed Marr's absolute mastery of the form. The strident acoustic opening and pounding bass prefaces one of Morrissey's most sincerely sarcastic vocal pleadings. The soothing first line, "Sweetness, I was only joking . . ." is followed by a succession of typically violent images, with Morrissey comparing himself to a modern-day Joan of Arc. The references to being bound at the stake and ostracized from the human race for his "big-mouthed" outbursts were amusingly topical, particularly in view of his recent catalogue of controversial remarks. The single added a witty, satirical edge to The Smiths' ever-improving songbook. Marr regarded the song as his Jumpin' Jack Flash, with as dextrous a display of Keith Richards-styled rhythm-playing as one could reasonably demand. The song even contained a heart-stopping "moment in time". Joyce's fierce, speaker-splitting drum roll followed by Marr's gambolling rhythmic break was an object lesson in the brilliant use of economy. The entire effect was complemented by the unexpected appearance of a "female" vocalist, who sang in perfect syncopation to Morrissey. Identified as "Ann Coates" (a play on Ancoats), the mystery vocalist was actually Morrissey himself, recorded at a faster speed by the mischievous Marr.

Although Bigmouth Strikes Again contained enough drama and commercial clout to threaten the Top 5, it slumped to an appalling Number 26, faring no better than Shakespeare's Sister and worse than The Boy With The Thorn In His Side. It was a frightening injustice, no doubt made worse by Travis's insistence that the forthcoming There Is A Light That Never Goes Out would have fared better. However, Marr had made a crucial point in establishing The Smiths as one of the few artistes of the '80s that crafted singles of supreme worth. He now looks back at those chart disappointments with resignation:

"I was happy to have certain songs on singles like Shakespeare's Sister, That Joke Isn't Funny Anymore and Bigmouth Strikes Again because they were radical rock singles, and that suited me. I was happy just owning them myself. The fact that we didn't get on Top Of The Pops with those records is neither here nor there. I preferred those to the ones that did get on television."

Nevertheless, at the time of their release, the group were unforgiving in their condemnation of Rough Trade's promotion, and the threat of defection to a major label remained ever present.

For all their acclaimed "Britishness", The Smiths never exuded that most British of traits: "reserve". Instead, they trumpeted their achievement loudly and immodestly. The cockiness of Marr and the self-adulation of Morrissey were translated into a group motto that read: "We're the most important group of the '80s." What might have sounded empty, self-satisfied arrogance in the mouths of lesser beings, served as an innocent statement of fact to Smiths aficionados. The Smiths used self-serving epithets as a form of party political broadcast and found that their boasts were rapidly transformed into critical cliché. The propaganda worked to spectacular effect encouraging insecure, fence-sitting journalists to trot out the "most important group of the '80s" line without seriously considering its full implications. By the summer of 1986, however, the need to justify The Smiths was rendered irrelevant.

The Queen Is Dead is the ultimate proof, if one were needed, of the complete legitimacy of The Smiths' unironic self-aggrandizement. Arguably the most accomplished album of the '80s, the work captures the Morrissey/Marr partnership at its apotheosis. More than any other work in their canon, The Queen Is Dead crystallized the contradictory and complementary visions of its creators in a panoramic sweep of absolute grandeur. An album of strikingly different tones, the work begins with the drama of a fully-fledged concept album and closes with a comic lightness of touch that could not have come from any other pen but that of Morrissey. The range of mood, emotion and perspective is breathtakingly diverse: rage and laughter alternates, sometimes within the space of a single line; romantic idealism gives way to Carry On comedy; maudlin despair is alleviated by music hall frivolity; humanity and misanthropy coalesce uneasily, while world-weary resignation finds expression through a strange yet glorious defiance.

On The Queen Is Dead, Morrissey emerges as the most interesting pop songwriter of his generation, with a variety of personae: the scathing satirist, the introspective romantic, the gauche comedian and the playfully ironic plagiarist. Marr's achievement is no less striking. The 19-year-old genius of yore is transformed into a mature wunderkind, whose work echoes the casually-cool rock classicism of Keith Richards, the brooding drama of mid-period Pete Townshend and the purist sensitivity of vintage Eric Clapton.

The Queen Is Dead borrowed its title from a section of Hubert Selby Jnr's notorious book Last Exit To Brooklyn. Within its new context, however, the homosexual angle is underplayed in favour of a mock-epic assault on Her Majesty The Queen. Significantly, the album was to be titled Margaret On A Guillotine, but Morrissey would not complete his anti-Thatcherite diatribe until 1987.

Retaining the political theme, he focused attention on the state of contemporary Britain. The atmospheric Cicely Courtneidge singalong brilliantly captures the evanescent image of an ill-defined but lost verdant England that dissolves before Joyce's fierce drumming and Marr's epically-constructed soundscape of MC5/Stooges-influenced wah-wah guitar. "Morrissey said he wanted to include Take Me Back To Dear Old Blighty on the track," Marr recalls. "But he wasn't to know that I was intending to lead into feedback and drum rolls. It was just magic. I got the drum riff going and Andy had the bass line, which was one of his best ever, and something that bass players still haven't matched. I went in there with all the lads watching, did the take and they just went, 'Wow'. I came out and I was shaking. When I suggested, 'I'll do it again', they just said, 'No way! No way!' "

What added to the song's tremendous power was Morrissey's startling vocal and fascinating lyrics. Scabrously satiric, he approaches the body politic armed with a scalpel that he will later turn unexpectedly on himself. No longer content merely to drop his trousers to the Queen, he now dreams of seeing her head in a sling. The fantasy execution, however, is superseded by a more convivial narrative. Unlike the agitprop Margaret On A Guillotine, The Queen Is Dead is playful and irreverent, rather than vicious and vindictive. Morrissey does not enter the palace clutching a hangman's noose, but chooses a harmless sponge and a rusty spanner.

Moreover, it soon transpires that his intention is not regicide but pleasant banter.* The virulent social critique of royal decadence, church materialism, public house escapism and pre-teen drug-pedalling presents a nightmare vision of a country weakened by spiritual and moral decay. "You can get florid about politics and the state of the country," he declared, "but it comes down to the very basic arguments that they don't care, and they should!" Warming to his theme, Morrissey launched a familiar attack on the monarchy: "The royal family is an institution which is built entirely on murder and deceit and fraud and hate and we should never forget those things. We shouldn't feel that simply because it's an English tradition that it's good."

What is interesting about The Queen Is Dead, however, is that it transcends mere diatribe to focus on the personal. In what is undoubtedly his most serious, powerful and outward-looking Smiths song, Morrissey turns inward to relieve his rage and disillusionment with snatches of bathetic humour. The Queen's criticism of his singing prompts an amusingly self-deprecating reference to his non-musical abilities ("That's nothing, you should hear me play piano!"). The imaginary transvestitism of dear Charles displayed on the front page of the Daily Mail is mirrored by the singer's shock and shame at discovering skeletons in his own family tree ("I'm the 18th pale descendant of some old Queen or other"). What begins as an epic is continually subverted into mock epic; the rant becomes a romp and, finally, a black fairy tale. In the final stanza, Morrissey emerges as a reassuring town crier, proclaiming the death of the Queen before returning to more familiar introspective musings that tell him "life is very long when you're lonely".

Frankly Mr Shankly, which was mixed towards the end of The Queen Is Dead sessions, contrastingly evoked the

* This episode was inspired by the disturbed Michael Fagin, who not only broke into Buckingham Palace, but actually entered the Queen's boudoir and chatted with her over a cigarette, before being led away.

uproarious spirit of George Formby. Morrissey reveals himself as a music-hall humorist with one of the most cutting voices in pop history. It is generally acknowledged in music business circles that such lyrics as "I want to leave/You will not miss me/I want to go down in musical history" are an oblique reference to the Rough Trade dispute, with Travis cast in the central role as "righteous", "holy" and "a pain in the arse". Absent from the lyric sheet was the spiteful coda "Give us your money!" How did Travis feel about being labelled the butt of Morrissey's satiric wit? "Well, it's not a particularly charming thought, is it?" he responded. "There's a huge amount of humour in the song and I'm not really upset by it. Camp spite? I think there's a lot of that there, but I don't take it too seriously. Morrissey likes to have some fun and that's what rock'n'roll is about."

The ordering of the album tracks was carefully constructed so that the canter of Frankly Mr Shankly abruptly shifts to the desolate introspection of I Know It's Over. A candidate for Morrissey's most bleak work, the song laments the loss of a happiness that was itself a fantasy ("I know it's over/And it never really began"). Against a funereal melody, Morrissey's central image of being buried alive gains poignant force. Marr felt overwhelmed by Morrissey's vocal reading of the song, which he regards as one of his finest. "I'll never forget when he did it," he remembers. "It's one of the highlights of my life. It was that good, that strong. Every line he was hinting at where he was going to go. I kept thinking, 'Is he going to go there? Yes, he is!' It was just brilliant."

The speculations on loneliness and uncertainty in I Know It's Over continued on the elliptical Never Had No One Ever. In recalling the lack of ease in patrolling Manchester's streets, Morrissey presents life as a nightmare that lasted "20 years, seven months and 27 days". Strictly speaking, that would date life's awakening for Steven as January 18, 1980. Predictably, there was nothing special about that particular day, which he spent at home, nursing a sore foot, reading a copy of The Murderers' Who's Who and recalling a recent horrific spell as a hospital porter.

The central message of Never Had No One Ever was

repeated in the run-off grooves of the album, which read: "Fear of Manchester"/"Them Was Rotten Days".

The recollections of late '70s/early '80s Manchester culminate in the wonderfully witty Cemetry Gates*. Marr's sprightly arrangement expertly evokes the *joie de vivre* among the gravestones. The melody was conceived in Marr's kitchen one afternoon when he was tuning his guitar. Morrissey was struck by a particular run of chords and announced authoritatively: "That's the song!" Marr was impressed. "When I sat down my idea was for it to be a Kinks song," he explains. "For some reason, it was speeded-up. It's strange." No less strange to source-hunting aficionados were those playful lyrics. Given Morrissey's insistence, "If you must write prose/poems/the words you use should be your own/don't plagiarize or take 'on loan'," it seems sneakingly appropriate that he would choose this moment to indulge some of his legendary "borrowings".

The most moving stanza in the song is the cod Shakespearian soliloquy: "All those people, all those lives/Where are they now?/With loves, and hates/And passions just like mine/They were born/And then they lived/And then they died/Which seems so unfair/And I want to cry." The inspiration for these lines came from one of Morrissey's favourite films, The Man Who Came To Dinner. In the movie, Katharine Hepburn provides a similar philosophical lament: "All those people, all those lives, where are they now? Here was a woman who once lived and loved, full of the same passions, fears, jealousies, hates. And what remains of it now .. . I want to cry." The melancholic air that pervades the song is also the source of its exuberance. Literary oneupmanship is amusingly described in Morrissey's heretical placing of Wilde before such major poets as John Keats and W.B. Yeats. Other comic moments, such as the use of archaisms and crazy tense

* The misspelling of cemetery was not intentional. Morrissey always had problems with the word.

32

breakdowns ("'ere long done do does did") provide an engaging self-mockery. The underlying nostalgic mood gains further force from the real life memories of sunny days spent in Manchester's Southern Cemetery, where Morrissey and Linder played out their own version of the graveyard scene in Billy Liar.

The sublime single Bigmouth Strikes Again opens side two on a suitably emphatic note, buoyed by the light touch of The Boy With The Thorn In His Side and a further frolic of transvestitism in Vicar In A Tutu. Marr's rockabilly rhythms forge an unlikely link between the mid-'50s Memphis Sun sound and that quintessentially English phenomenon – the fabled, saucy vicar of Sunday tabloid infamy. The melody had emerged while Marr was riffing on some chords and Joyce casually joined in. Morrissey popped his head around the studio door and exclaimed: "Carry on! That's the song." As Joyce noted: "If we'd have had a name producer I don't think Vicar In A Tutu would have come about."

Comedy again gives way to melodrama with the anthemic There Is A Light That Never Goes Out, on which Marr displays his arranging abilities, courtesy of some subtly swirling strings. The song delicately describes the painful yearning for a sensual/sexual experience which seems doomed to remain tantalizingly ungraspable, even when the chance is offered. Morrissey's ultimate expression of adolescent wish-fulfilment, the composition dramatizes a seductive longing for a romantic death ("And if a double-decker bus/Crashes into us/To die by your side/Is such a heavenly way to die") whose pathetic futility might bring immortal meaning to a fantasy relationship.

After the high melodrama of There Is A Light That Never Goes Out, The Smiths close the album with the bathetic Some Girls Are Bigger Than Others. On the previous two albums, the final tracks mourned murder and animal slaughter, but here Morrissey breaks with tradition to lighten the tone. In citing Anthony And Cleopatra, Morrissey does not borrow from Shakespeare, but prefers the uproarious film Carry On Cleo, in which actor Sid James is shown cracking open a bottle of ale. As the song fades, Morrissey revisits the early '60s for a muted reprise of Johnny Tillotson's Send Me The Pillow You Dream On. This purposely unportentous finale, with some excellent slide work from Marr, supplies a playful coda to an album of classic distinction. The Queen Is Dead was a magnificent achievement that would transcend its time to lodge at the summit of those deceptively mutable "Critics' All-Time Top 100 Albums".

The contribution of the rhythm section to the longevity of the work deserves special commendation, as Marr is quick to note. "There was perfect musical unity between myself, Mike and Andy," he stresses. "Mike really learned to play with me like no one else. I really felt I turned him on to the Charlie Watts ethic. It was a dream for me to play on. Mike was just behind me and Andy fitted in the middle. That's the way we worked. Mike learned to be a good drummer by playing in The Smiths. I had something playing with Mike and Andy that I won't have playing with any other people."

HICKORY WIND

The Life And Times Of Gram Parsons

BEN FONG-TORRES

Even when alive, Gram Parsons was a lost hero; his mysterious death in 1973 (aged just 27) merely ensured that his cult status would last forever. Talented, handsome, free-spirited and troubled, his music (as a solo act and with the International Submarine Band, The Flying Burrito Brothers and, briefly, The Byrds) was among the first to span the chasm between rock and country. Though he never achieved commercial success, Parsons has influenced rafts of artists including The Rolling Stones, The Eagles, Elvis Costello and, most recently, The Lemonheads. Fong-Torres's book attempts to make sense of this most romantic yet unfulfilled life. The extract that follows finds Parsons, in the Spring of 1968, replacing David Crosby in The Byrds and setting his new colleagues on the road to country rock. At least, that was the plan . . .

GRAM PARSONS WASN'T exactly bursting with credentials when he came up for consideration as a member of The Byrds after David Crosby was fired in 1968.

His first album was flopping; he wrote a song that Peter Fonda recorded, and he had a few flickers of a bit part in The Trip. He was just the kind of dilettante that a guy like Chris Hillman should have snubbed.

Chris was the genuine article. He was from the San Diego

area and had gotten into folk music, as most young people had, through Pete Seeger and The Weavers. But, while most college kids of the early '60s, wary of juke-box pop, fell for the Sta-Prest folk music of the Kingston Trio and the New Christy Minstrels, Chris made another left turn – into the bluegrass music of Flatt and Scruggs and the Gosdin Brothers.

Chris took up the mandolin, played local country music television shows, and got good enough at age 16 to join The Golden State Boys, a bluegrass institution in Southern California, where he played alongside bassist-singer Rex Gosdin and guitarist-singer Vern Gosdin. When the Gosdins made a shift toward folk music, they renamed themselves the Hillmen. Their producer, Jim Dickson, moved on to co-manage a fledgling band called The Jet Set. When The Jet Set members found themselves in need of a bass player, Jim thought of Chris, even though he'd never played the instrument. Chris, who in 1964 was languishing, working for one of the folkie ensembles created by Christy Minstrels founder Randy Sparks, took the offer. Soon enough, The Jet Set became The Byrds.

Now, in March 1968, the band was a mess. Having lost original members Gene Clark and David Crosby, they were down to three. And, after completing their first post-Crosby album, The Notorious Byrd Brothers, they saw drummer Mike Clarke leave. The Byrds drafted Chris's cousin, Kevin Kelley. Now, with tour dates lined up, they were desperately looking for a new member when Chris remembered Gram Parsons.

They had met a few months earlier. "We had on the same kind of jeans and the same looks on our faces," Gram said in late 1972. Chris had heard of Gram; had heard some of the Submarine Band. And they had the same business manager: Larry Spector.

Chris brought Gram to a rehearsal studio, where Roger McGuinn, founder and leader of The Byrds, was thinking about hiring a piano player who could handle jazz as well as rock. He was still in an Eight Miles High mood, so he asked Gram if he could play some jazz. Gram, as he recalled, faked a blues figure of some sort, sang, played some guitar, and seemed like a nice guy who'd fit in with the band. Roger, in classic '60s, laissez-faire style, hired him on the spot. "I had no idea he was Hank Williams, Jr.," he said.

That remark was a trimmed-down, '90s version of the dilly of a comment Roger gave the rock magazine Fusion in the early '70s: "We just hired a piano player and he turned out to be Parsons, a monster in sheep's clothing. And he exploded out of this sheep's clothing. God! It's George Jones! In a sequin suit!"

Chris, thinking back, doesn't know how Gram got hired. The Byrds needed a tenor singer and an instrumentalist, preferably a keyboard player. Instead, they got a lead vocalist, a so-so-rhythm guitarist, and, once Gram and Chris found their common ground, yet another musical direction.

Country was hardly foreign to The Byrds. A year before Gram's arrival, and months before he was making the ISB album, The Byrds had Clarence White, The Kentucky Colonels' hot guitarist, playing on Time Between on their Younger Than Yesterday album. In 1965, The Byrds, at Chris Hillman's suggestion, recorded Satisfied Mind, the Porter Wagoner hit of the mid-'50s.

Having gone from folk-rock to psychedelic music to electronic space sounds, McGuinn was thinking about a two-album set in which The Byrds would traverse nothing less than the history of 20th-century music, beginning with traditional mountain music and ending, of course, electronically, state-of-the-future.

But his new Byrd put an end to that.

Gram, said Roger, had a "burning thing" for a contemporary take on country music – "to blend The Beatles and country; to really do something revolutionary. Gram thought we could win over the country audience. He figured, once they dig you, they never let go."

The Byrds' leader not only bought the pitch – lock, stock, and with both barrels blazing – he began listening to nothing but country radio stations. After Byrds shows, he said, the guys would go straight to the country music bars. Roger went to Nudie's and got properly outfitted. He even bought a Cadillac. "It was like an adventure."

Soon, the band decided to cut its next album in Nashville – Music City, USA. And not only would they be the first long-haired folk-rock band from California to invade Nashville, they would crash the temple of all that was good and backward about country music: The Grand Ole Opry.

After rehearsals, The Byrds flew into Nashville for a week of sessions beginning on March 9 at the CBS Studios at Sixteenth and Hawkins Street (since renamed Music Square East and Music Circle South), a block away from the Country Music Hall of Fame. They were to work with producer Gary Usher, who'd steered them through the Younger Than Yesterday and The Notorious Byrd Brothers albums.

To help authenticate The Byrds' country efforts, Usher hired session players from Nashville, including steel guitarists J.D. Maness (who was on the ISB album) and Lloyd Green, and string bassist Roy M. Huskey (a veteran of sessions with, among many others, Lee Hazlewood). Clarence White, who'd been an uncredited sideman with The Byrds since Crosby's departure, signed on, as did John Hartford on fiddle and banjo, and Earl Ball (another ISB session player) on piano. Ex-Submarine Band drummer Jon Corneal also played.

At their first session, the Byrds recorded Bob Dylan's You Ain't Goin' Nowhere and a song Gram had written with Bob Buchanan, Hickory Wind.

Meantime, Columbia had convinced The Grand Ole Opry's producers to let The Byrds on the show, on the very next night. At only 21 years old, Gram would be performing in country music's mecca. They would be guests in the half-hour slot hosted by Tompall Glaser and the Glaser Brothers. Years later, Tompall would emerge, along with Waylon Jennings, Willie Nelson, and Kris Kristofferson, as one of Nashville's "outlaw" country artists, singing and writing tough, rock-based music that rolled far away from the Music Row mainstream.

For now, The Byrds were in the mother church of country music, and they didn't need to be told to be on their best behaviour. The Grand Ole Opry, started up in 1925, was the most powerful vehicle for country music from the '40s through the '60s, with its 50,000-watt clear-channel signal reaching out from WSM, its flagship station in Nashville, to 30 states every Saturday night. It was a tightly run ship. When Hank Williams, who'd exploded on to the Ryman Auditorium stage with a debut that earned six encore calls, began missing shows, the Opry fired him.

It seems right that the Opry, since 1943, had been produced out of the Ryman, which was built as a tabernacle in 1912, and which still offered seating in long, curved, wooden pews and no air conditioning. On summer evenings, the Opry handed out paper fans.

On the evening of March 10, 1968, things were decidedly cool. Tompall Glaser gave The Byrds a big build-up, making sure to say that the boys were on Columbia Records and that they were singing a real country tune, Merle Haggard's Sing Me Back Home, with Tennessee's own Gram Parsons on lead vocals.

Homegrown or not, Gram and The Byrds looked like spacemen to the audience. But, good Southerners most of them, they offered a polite hand. Some hooted at the band. Chris heard shouts of "Tweet-tweet!' and "Cut your hair!" But the audience warmed up when they found that these weirdos from out West could actually play.

After the first song, Tompall strode out, leading the applause. The Byrds had told the Opry that their second number would be Life In Prison, so Glaser cued them: "Well, now you're going to do another Merle Haggard song, aren't you?"

Gram took the microphone. "We're not going to do that tonight," he said, taking everyone on stage and behind the scenes by surprise. "We're going to do a song for my grandmother, who used to listen to The Grand Ole Opry with me when I was little. It's a song I wrote, called Hickory Wind."

The other Byrds looked at each other. They had gotten stoned backstage, and they weren't ready for a plot twist like this. They just managed to catch up with Gram, and the song proceeded smoothly.

Even as he sang, Gram could see, off to the side of the stage, the Opry's reaction. "The Glaser brothers just flipped out," he said. "They were yelling at us from off stage and stomping up and down. Roy Acuff [*the 'King of the Cowboys,' who joined the Opry in 1938*] was having fits."

After the two-song set, The Byrds strode by a crew of hostile Opry producers and staffers. Tompall Glaser collared Chris and yelled: "You made me look like a fool on the radio." Meanwhile, Skeeter Davis, who'd had her own skirmishes with Opry officials, ran over to The Byrds and greeted them with kisses. Said Gram: "She was so happy that somebody had finally blown those guys off."

In the audience, few knew that anything untoward had happened. But, as Roger McGuinn reminded me, the Opry was a controlled broadcast environment, complete with applause signs. Light them up and they'd clap. Shut them off and they'd shut up.

Gram's aunt Pauline, who was there with her mother and several other family members and friends, was unaware that anything was wrong. From where she sat, everybody loved The Byrds. As for Gram breaking format and upsetting the Opry, she responded with a rhetorical question: "Don't you think that was typical of him? He did what you didn't expect."

Chris figured that all Gram did was make his dream come true. "He took the reins. He was right smack into that – 'Here I am on the Opry. I'm Hank Williams!' – so he went with it. He played the whole role out."

Returning to the CBS studio, The Byrds cut Woody Guthrie's Pretty Boy Floyd on Monday, the traditional I Am A Pilgrim the next day, and wrapped up their week with another Dylan song, Nothing Was Delivered. Gram invited Grandma Nancy and Aunt Pauline and her kids to one session, proudly introducing them to The Byrds and some of the side musicians. Gram and several of the other Byrds also visited her house for a late supper.

Gram clearly enjoyed being home. The South had not been kind to him, but in the song he'd dedicated to his grandmother, Gram addressed its tug-and-pull:

> It's a hard way to find out
> That trouble is real
> In a faraway city, with a faraway feel
> But it makes me feel better
> Each time it begins
> Callin' me home, hickory wind

Hickory Wind, simply structured as it was – three verses, no chorus – was one of Gram's finest moments as a songwriter. He wrote the song on a train, on his way back to Los Angeles from Florida in early 1968. In Coconut Grove, where he'd gone to see Fred Neil, he'd run into Bob Buchanan, the former Christy Minstrels member whom he'd met in LA, who was also visiting Fred. Bob and Gram decided to ride back to LA together. On the Santa Fe Super Chief, the two men stayed mostly to themselves – Gram was having problems with Nancy, and Bob was having problems with drugs – until Gram pulled out a guitar and asked Bob to help out with a song he was writing.

Gram had the first verse down, recalling oak trees in South Carolina that he used to climb and establishing the hickory wind as a nostalgic symbol of his youth in the South.

But he needed a second verse. Bob drew on their common experiences in the music business in LA and came up with a second verse based on their experiences there, and the hollowness even its promised riches and pleasures could bring.

They worked together on the final verse, about a distant city with a distant feel. That, to Bob, was the key. "That's the theme of the song: it's pretty damned rough trying to make it in the city, with all the business and bullshit."

What made the song so universal was its recognition of one of life's big questions – Is that all there is? – combined with pleasant evocations of youth and the safety a kid felt being at home among the pines, the oak, and the brush. All recalled by the gentle sound, even if it's only in one's mind, of a hickory wind.

AFTER WRAPPING UP the sessions in Music City, The Byrds took off for a tour of East Coast colleges. Buoyed by a standing ovation at MIT, the band returned to Los Angeles in early April for their West Coast debut, in the form of a farewell party for their former publicist, Derek Taylor, whose clients included the Monterey Pop Festival, A&M Records, and The Beatles. For the farewell, The Byrds chose to play the Hollywood club in which they'd made their debut three years before: Ciro's.

Rolling Stone magazine's LA correspondent, Jerry Hopkins, was there, and filed a report giving Gram his first ink in what was emerging as the rock world's most important journal.

In the story, Gram was referred to as "Graham Parsons", but he got an endorsement from McGuinn: "Graham's bag is country and we're going to let him do his thing, and support him and work together on things." Gram also got a good review: "They appear secure in the country milieu," Hopkins wrote about their set at Ciro's. "Graham sings often and he sings well, sharing 'lead voice' with Roger."

In Los Angeles, The Byrds completed the Sweetheart Of The Rodeo sessions with a Tim Hardin song, Reputation; the traditional British ballad Pretty Polly; the two Haggard songs Life In Prison and Sing Me Back Home; another country standard, You're Still On My Mind; two songs suggested by Gram, You Don't Miss Your Water and the Louvin Brothers' The Christian Life; and two more songs written by Gram, One Hundred Years From Now and Lazy Days (the song that had been rejected for The Trip).

In early May, The Byrds took off for Europe, where they played two concerts at the site of the former underground mecca, Middle Earth, in Covent Garden. Gram was on electric piano and rhythm guitar; to underline the country sound, Doug Dillard played banjo. Among the audience were Mick Jagger and his girlfriend, the singer Marianne Faithfull.

The Byrds had shared concert bills with the Stones, and in London, Mick and Keith had played host to The Byrds. Keith was unaware of any personnel changes. "I went to see McGuinn," he said.

Roger remembered going out to Stonehenge with the other Byrds and Mick and Keith. It was a wet, blustery night, and the musicians passed a bottle of Johnny Walker Red around to fight the cold during the long trek out to the monument. The Byrds got so soaked that night that, while they were having breakfast, Mick sent a driver out to buy them socks.

Sometime during the visit to the monument, Roger told the Stones about The Byrds' plans to play in South Africa after another London engagement in July.

Miriam Makeba, the South African folk singer, had suggested that Roger go to her native country and witness apartheid – the governmental policy keeping blacks separated from whites – for himself.

Roger was a seeker. He wanted to know about things firsthand. He knew that fellow entertainers had boycotted the country, but after making inquiries, he received assurances that The Byrds would be playing to both black and white people. He naively interpreted that to mean mixed audiences, and he thought that he'd be striking a blow against apartheid.

The Stones didn't argue with Roger about his plans, but he remembered them getting on to Gram about it. Gram, at 21, was already listening hard to the more worldly, 24-year-old Keith Richards.

Between the two "Middle Earth" concerts, The Byrds flew to Rome and played the Piper Club. The shows were a knockout, but as they flew back to Los Angeles, they were headed for trouble. And, having met The Rolling Stones, Gram had more than a little stardust in his eyes.

LEE HAZLEWOOD HAD worked hard to establish his first record company, and he didn't like watching the Submarine Band falling apart just as its first album was being issued. Nor did he appreciate the leader of that band wandering off to another group. He decided to get hard-nosed.

He contacted CBS Records to inform the company that LHI Productions still owned the rights to Gram's vocal performances, if not to his compositions or to his work as an instrumentalist.

On the album Sweetheart Of The Rodeo, Gram had sung lead vocals on The Christian Life, You Don't Miss Your Water, Hickory Wind, and several others. After Lee's call, Columbia ordered Gram's voice stripped off the album and replaced by Roger's and Chris's. Roger got to work putting his own voice – with a brand-new Southern accent – where Gram's had been.

Gram, who admitted that his release from LHI was "kind of shaky" – that is, he marched into LHI's offices one day and simply announced that he was going with The Byrds – was upset with the results. On at least one track, The Christian Life, his voice was left on, he said, but "way in the background, as a guide to go by; it didn't work."

As Emmylou Harris told writer Alanna Nash, in her book, Behind Closed Doors: "If you listen real close in the headset, you can hear him. His phrasing is so different from Roger McGuinn's. It's like hearing a ghost, because his phrasing is the real traditional, Louvin Brothers phrasing, and Roger McGuinn sang it like, you know, Roger McGuinn. And there's such an over-lapping that you can hear him in the spaces where Roger doesn't sing, because Gram elongates his phrasing."

Gram thought the strange mix "gave it too much of the old Byrds sound, which we were fighting against – not because it wasn't any good, but because there was all this other stuff to work with, and we didn't need to look back, as Bob Dylan once sort of said."

Producer Gary Usher also dropped three cuts: Pretty Polly, which Gram had picked for his daughter Polly, and on which Roger sang lead; Reputation, with Gram on lead vocals; and Gram's Lazy Days, again with Gram up front. Although CBS and LHI resolved the legal matter, those tracks stayed off the album. "We were just about to scratch Hickory Wind when somebody ran in with a piece of paper," said Gram. "That's the last one they had saved."

On another occasion, Gram said that the sessions went well – until the threat from LHI. "They had to pull a few things out of the can that weren't supposed to be used, things like Life In Prison and (An Empty Bottle, A Broken Heart, And) You're Still On My Mind. We just did them as warm-up numbers. We could've done them a lot better . . . They just chopped up the album however they wanted to."

Gram blamed Roger: "He erased it and did the vocals himself and fucked it up," he told Cameron Crowe in early 1973. In another interview, he blamed Gary Usher. "The producer decided it should go Hollywood freaky, and it wasn't the time for that. I thought it was the time for a Nashville Skyline or something like the album as I remember it, a serious country album. It was a great album that might as well have never been recorded. So there's another Sweetheart Of The Rodeo, and, uh, I dig it."

Gary, who died of cancer in 1990, claimed that the threat of a lawsuit had no bearing on the album. Speaking in 1988 with The Cosmic American Music News, the magazine of the Gram Parsons Memorial Foundation, the producer said Roger did overdub some songs because of legal problems, but that the differences were resolved while the group was in Nashville, "so whoever sang leads on the songs . . . were there because that's how we wanted to slice the album up." Roger, he said, was wary "that Parsons was getting a little bit too much out of this thing . . . He didn't want the album to turn into a Gram Parsons album."

Terry Melcher, the early Byrds' producer who later worked with Gram, said Gram deeply resented Roger for what happened with Sweetheart and bore a grudge for years.

Both Roger and Chris disputed Gary Usher's version of events. Roger insisted that there was a legal problem, that all of Gram's lead vocals had to be erased, and that when the problem was resolved, Gram restored his vocals. Roger's was left on some tracks, but, he pointed out, he'd redone Hickory Wind, and Gram wound up with the lead vocal on it.

With the album finally completed, The Byrds returned to

London in July for "Sounds '68," a charity concert at the Albert Hall, headlined by The Move and including The Easybeats, Bonzo Dog Doo Dah Band, and a young white soul singer named Joe Cocker. But it was The Byrds, who kicked their set off with a searing So You Want To Be A Rock 'n' Roll Star, who stole the show. The New Musical Express added "Grahm" Parsons to the growing list of misspellings, but reporter Nick Logan reported: "A good section of the 4,000 audience was there to see them alone, and they let them know it."

With their popularity in Europe happily reconfirmed, The Byrds prepared to leave for their next engagements – all in South Africa – when Gram announced that he would not be going.

In a statement to Melody Maker, Gram said he'd been thinking about the issue of South Africa's policy of apartheid for some time. "I first heard about the South African tour two months ago," he said. "I knew right off when I heard about it that I didn't want to go. I stood firmly on my conviction."

"It was total garbage," said Chris, who flew into a rage when Gram deserted the band. "I really wanted to murder him," he said. He was certain that Gram simply wanted to hang out with Mick and Keith. "They were filling his head, I'm sure, with stories about South Africa."

They were. Almost from the moment they met, said Keith, Gram was confiding in him.

"I've got something I want to talk to you about," Gram began. "Maybe you can help me." He told Keith about The Byrds' plans and added, "I have a funny feeling about it and I don't know much about it. What's the deal with South Africa?"

"Well," Keith remembered telling Gram, "it's like when you were growing up down South, if you were the wrong colour. It's exactly the same."

Later – possibly at Stonehenge, or at Mick's flat on Chester Square afterwards – Gram asked Mick and Keith point-blank whether he should drop out of the trip to South Africa. Keith said: "Well, let me put it this way: *We* wouldn't go." And that settled it.

"I was instrumental in his leaving The Byrds," said Keith, "because I said, 'Nobody goes to play South Africa.'"

Gram later said that his hatred of racial segregation dated much further back than his last cup of tea with the Stones.

"Something a lot of people don't know about me is that I was brought up with a Negro for a brother," he said. "Like all Southern families, we had maids and servants, a whole family called the Dixons that took care of us. Sammy Dixon was a little older than me, and he lived with and grew up with me, so I learned at a real close level that segregation was just not it."

Aside from the slight overstatement about all Southern families having servants, Gram was reaching a bit when he recalled his occasional baby-sitter as a "brother"; none of his childhood playmates recalled Sammy being around.

However sincere Gram might have been, few who knew him believed him. Besides his attachment to the Stones, theories on why he pulled out ranged from his anger at Roger over Sweetheart Of The Rodeo to an increasing fear of flying – the trip to Johannesburg required a stopover in the Canary Islands, off the coast of Morocco, for refuelling – to one advanced by Carlos Bernal, a Byrds roadie who was pressed into service as a guitarist.

Gram dropped out, he said, "because he couldn't have things just exactly how he wanted them . . . He wanted a steel guitar to do a lot of his tunes. He wanted things that the band wasn't prepared to jump into overnight. So Gram didn't make it to the airport."

The South African tour was a disaster physically, mentally, musically, and politically. The tour, Chris conceded, "was a stupid farce and he [Gram] was right. We shouldn't have gone. But he shouldn't have let us down by copping out at the end."

On their return, and after recovering from his exhaustion, Roger announced a replacement for Gram: Clarence White. It was August, and Gram Parsons had been a Byrd for just over four months.

At the end of the month, CBS released Sweetheart Of The Rodeo with an ad showing the band – Gram included – behind a half-height brick wall on which was scrawled a too-neat graffito: THIS COUNTRY'S FOR THE BYRDS.

Rolling Stone gave Sweetheart a lukewarm review in its September 14 issue. Critic Barry Gifford suggested that no purist country fans listen to the "affectedly-straight C&W" effort. He left Gram unmentioned and judged the band's overall performance "simple, relaxed and folky". His final line: "It ought to make the 'Easy Listening' charts. 'Bringing it all back home' has never been an easy thing to do."

The review drove Jon Landau, Rolling Stone's chief music essayist, to his typewriter. He singled out The Byrds as the most consistently appreciative of country music among various rock bands dipping into the music.

Compared to Buffalo Springfield, Jon wrote, "The Byrds have approached country music as an entity in itself and have aimed for a greater degree of fidelity to the rules of the style." He praised Gram Parsons and various Nashville session players, and he concluded, as if in response to Barry: "The Byrds, in doing country as country, show just how powerful and relevant unadorned country music is to the music of today. And they leave just enough rock in the drums to let you know that they can still play rock'n'roll. That's what I call bringing it all back home."

Musically, Sweetheart was on solid ground. "The Byrds have always jumped around in different forms," Jon noted. "Every Byrds album is like an audio magazine containing the things that interest us at the moment."

But rock fans rejected the album. Sweetheart sold less than 50,000 and was The Byrds' poorest-selling album to date.

In 1968, the most uproarious year of the '60s, with 10,000 dead in Vietnam, campus revolts, King and Kennedy assassinated, the riots in Watts and Chicago, and the continuing wars against wars, young people were ripping and burning symbols of the Establishment everywhere. If any music form represented the straight world, it was country – even if it was being played by dope smokers.

Forget educated arguments about the purity of the music.

Forget its embrace by the Spoonful, the Springfield, and Bob Dylan. Forget that Jann Wenner, editor of Rolling Stone, in a persuasive essay in 1968, stated, "There is no question that rock and roll is connected with much of the country and western tradition" – and went further: "The soul music tradition has been deeply involved with country sounds; they are both from the South, and the marriage of the two is what was called rock'n'roll. In many ways it is the music of reconciliation, of people who have been wronged or wronged others, but who, in the end, found out that that's the way it is."

But in 1968, country music, to most left-thinking hipsters, was backwood, hillbilly, rednecks – in short, square. Kind of like Ralph Emery, the Nashville DJ who slapped at The Byrds when they were in town, and whom The Byrds slapped back, by way of a Gram Parsons composition, in Drug Store Truck Driving Man.

The Byrds, however, felt the longest sting. Going country, Roger concluded, was a bad move. The band never attracted the country audience it hoped to gain, and it lost a good part of its rock following.

What Roger forgot was the album itself. Flawed as it was, Sweetheart Of The Rodeo was a musical landmark, a statement that few others could make. For their daring as well as for their music, The Byrds have been rewarded with induction into the Rock and Roll Hall of Fame, and Columbia issued a four-CD retrospective of The Byrds in 1990, including several of the lost Sweetheart tracks featuring Gram Parsons on lead vocals.

On its own, the Sweetheart album has worn well through the years, and even inspired a young female country act to name itself Sweethearts Of The Rodeo.

Roger admits that, in recent years, Sweetheart has become a classic. "It was picked by Rolling Stone as one of the Top 200 albums of the last 25 years," he noted.

But back when it counted, Sweetheart was ignored. The album stalled at Number 77 on the Billboard album charts. The Byrds' previous album, The Notorious Byrd Brothers, peaked at Number 47. Before that, Fifth Dimension and its follow-up,

Younger Than Yesterday, had hit Number 24.

In the summer of 1968, all Gram Parsons meant to Roger was trouble. In South Africa, Roger had barely survived a near nervous breakdown.

Meanwhile, Gram went with Keith and his common-law wife, actress Anita Pallenberg, to Redlands, Keith's country house in West Wittering, a village 90 minutes Southwest of London on the coast of the English Channel.

Here the Okefenokee Kid and the Dartford Devil traded licks and forged a friendship. And when Gram returned to Los Angeles in August, he was accompanied by Keith and Anita. At the airport, they were met in style by a car and driver.

The driver was Phil Kaufman.

UP-TIGHT

The Velvet Underground Story

VICTOR BOCKRIS/GERARD MALANGA

Up-Tight is the insiders' story of Andy Warhol's Factory and The Velvet Underground, consisting mainly of interviews with those who were there. In this extract, featuring input from all the band and Victor Bockris (author), Gerard Malanga (dancer), Paul Morrissey (filmmaker), Nat Finkelstein (photographer), Ronnie Cutrone (painter), Chris Stein (later of Blondie) and Betsey Johnson (model), the group's most famous album, The Velvet Underground And Nico, is recalled and discussed.

NICO HAD ALWAYS been a problem. She wanted to sing all the songs. What was she supposed to do when she wasn't singing? Looked at from today it seems just right – the tall, thin hauntingly beautiful blonde in a white suit standing in front of four thin guys (it took people some time to catch on that Maureen was a . . . chick) in black wearing sunglasses – but then, Nico was uptight. She didn't have anything to do. She felt uncomfortable just standing there. Why couldn't she sing more songs? Nico was always very unhappy. Everybody was uptight. Lou was always jealous of her. It all came to a head one day when he stormed into the Factory screaming, "So she photographs great in high contrast black and white, I'm not playing with her any more!" The record's release had been delayed. A special machine had to be made to make the original cover, on which the banana peeled. Zappa's Mothers Of Invention's Freak Out record had already been released.

Nico was still playing downstairs in the small bar called Stanley's. She stood behind the bar backed by an acoustic guitar. Sterling says that he, John and Lou took turns as did Rambling Jack Elliott, Tim Hardin (whom Paul called "Tim Heroin"), Tim Buckley, and Jackson Browne, who was living with Nico on Columbus Avenue at 81st Street. They still ran the films behind her. Paul Morrissey was pushing Nico's solo career. The press continued to pay attention to the "Andy Warhol Superstar". Paul was always trying to persuade Nico to stop taking drugs. Among other personalities on the scene an earnest Leonard Cohen attended her every performance, and later made use of some of her techniques on his own recordings. By the time The Velvet Underground And Nico Produced by Andy Warhol (which is how the first album is represented) was released in March, 1967, The Exploding Plastic Inevitable was naturally dissolving.

BOCKRIS: How were you feeling when the record came out?
TUCKER: I was very excited. I ran out to the store and bought one.
BOCKRIS: Didn't they give you a copy?
TUCKER: Oh yeah, but I wanted to buy one. Finding it in stores was nice, but that didn't last long because MGM fucked up. They didn't really distribute it at all. But I was very excited, and Sterling was too, as I recall, and I'm sure John and Lou were thrilled.
MORRISON: I was never more excited about anything, and used to call up Cashbox to find out our chart position before the magazine hit the stands. I couldn't wait to know.
BOCKRIS: What were you doing in March?
TUCKER: I lived on Long Island, so I didn't really hang out much, because they were all in the city. I don't think Sterling and Lou did that much socializing really. They might meet at Max's by chance, but they didn't hang out together that much.
MORRISON: We lived close by, and were together most of the time. We went to Max's every night that we were in town. That's where our friends were.

MORRISSEY: As soon as the record came out the Velvets didn't want to work any more. They thought they became very famous when their album was finally released. I think they just wanted to separate from Andy, although we went on tour with them all over the country! I forget who booked that tour but God Almighty I could never forget that gruelling ordeal on the buses. We were going on buses! We got all these bookings.

The success of Chelsea Girls, which was now showing in a major theatre in New York, had drawn Andy and Paul into the movie business. During '66 they had spent little time filming anything except Chelsea Girls, focusing the majority of their time on The E.P.I. Now as Andy began the incessant filming that was to lead to the 24-hour movie released at the end of '67, the focus of his attention was shifting. In essence they had done everything they could with the rock'n'roll genre – in the space of one year isolated and frozen for inspection several groundbreaking ideas – and they could see that any further collaboration was not going to lead to anything different.

MORRISON: Antonioni wanted to use us as the band in the rock club sequence in Blow-Up, and we were more than willing. However, the expense of bringing the whole entourage to England proved too much for him. The sequence was one of the last things to be shot in the film, and he was running low on funds. So he used The Yardbirds doing a Who impersonation.

MALANGA: Are you surprised by the longevity of the Velvets now?

MORRISSEY: I am in a way, but I do think it was good music, it was a good album, it was different, it was unusual, I think most of the songs were really good. They certainly were an innovation, but you know we went on tour with them, I was a manager of the goddamn thing for almost a year or more and I remember, because they never released the album, but once the album came out I think that's when they wanted to go off and be themselves, and not have any revenue go back to Andy and me, and they didn't want to do anything. They said they didn't want to work and suddenly the whole thing was over. The album didn't take off or anything right away.

BOCKRIS: What was Andy's take on working with the Velvets?

CUTRONE: It was great for Andy because he got a totally captive audience to watch such films as Eat and Sleep, whereas before the general public would see it as a curio, last 20 minutes into the film and split, or sit it out just to be cool. Now here was a way to display his films – the boring ones are great classics but they're still boring – and have an audience totally captive watching a man eat an apple in a rocking chair. That was a giant breakthrough.

BOCKRIS: Was their career largely based on intuition?

CUTRONE: I think it was largely as unspoken as possible, because you have to remember that being cool then was really important. And you couldn't blow your cool ever. You were not allowed to be a human being even. Everything worked through guilt and paranoia and through what feels best and what looks best that night. It was pretty much surface. I mean, however deep and intense the music was. One of Andy's famous quotes from that period is, "Your worst reviews are your best reviews." So, from the I-will-not-budge-an-inch attitude, their bad reviews were the kind of publicity that set the Velvets apart from anybody else. From a dollars-and-cents point of view that was not too cool. That was just like, you know, "Uh, uh, we hope we make some money here too." So there were mixed feelings about the critical reactions. The Velvets always got put down but instantly other groups started recognizing that art sometimes goes with music and they could really cash in on captivating an audience in the particular way and giving them not only music but visuals, and then it just took off.

MALANGA: There was always a problem between Lou and John ultimately when it came to who was the leader of the group.

MORRISSEY: Well, you know, I don't think so. I think John

idolized Lou. And he thought anything Lou said was wonderful and Lou knew. And when Lou was against Nico, John was a thousand times against Nico 100 per cent. In the end, Andy's connection with The Velvet Underground, like anything that happens to Andy, just made a gold-mine of good fortune for him and he became identified with rock and roll and the young generation. So, in a way, it was the best thing that ever happened to Andy to connect with a group that became that well-known. So, in a way, it was a very good thing that happened to him. But I did it hoping to make some money. Do you remember we went to a place in Detroit with Dick Clark and they gave us a check, it was a two-party check, and I never could collect the 2,500 dollars, because it had only one signature on it? Oh, it was all so awful, that life. I always felt sorry for rock and rollers afterwards – what a horrible life they lead running around to these horrible things. But we worked with the Velvets from the beginning for pure commercial reasons.

IT IS ONE of the paradoxes of Warhol's career that he is constantly criticized for being too much of a business man to be an artist, and that his major motivation is money. After doing great innovative work in a field, he often immediately left it for others to reap the sometimes great financial benefits. This was particularly true in his film work (ie My Hustler in terms of its influence on John Schlesinger's very successful Midnight Cowboy). Warhol's films deserve the highest praise for doing the ultimate in art – making people see life differently, as it really is. His work during 1966 in rock, where he literally created the light show and developed the whole multimedia dimension that was gobbled up by every conceivable rock entrepreneur, is still hardly credited in the plethora of rock histories that have been published.

The Velvets had made a great record, and were at the vortex of the most creative scene in New York when it came out, but they were not feeling as great as we might imagine. MGM was trying to do something new with its Verve label by bringing out some freaky records, but everybody got uptight when it was noticed that The Mothers Of Invention's Freak Out album was getting all the publicity. MGM either didn't understand the Velvets, or were censoring their subject matter and sound. It's also true, however, that Zappa had a rock'n'roll manager, Herb Cohen, who was experienced at working with music industry executives, whereas Warhol and Morrissey were not. The group sorely needed some business muscle in the music industry which is where they were getting ignored. While the E.P.I. had a good electrician who knew how to work a fuse-box, a good roadie, good projectionists, good dancers, good photographers, great musicians and fabulous art directors, The Velvet Underground didn't have anyone who really just wanted to be a good business person for them, which is probably the major factor in the faltering momentum of The E.P.I./Velvet Underground that became apparent. But then again, even if they had been able to get the gritty business together, they'd really done what they set out to do.

In the face of this total lack of support from their record label, The E.P.I. once again joined forces and played Rhode Island School Of Design. On April 11 they returned to the scene of their first real triumph, the University Of Michigan in Ann Arbor, where they played for the Architecture School. At a party after the show a young man called Jim Osterburg, aka Iggy Pop, caught his first glimpse of the Velvets, Andy and Nico who was playing with them again.

In April, the son of the Dom's Polish owner approached Andy with an idea for a new club in New York. Originally a Czechoslovakian health and social club in the East 70s, it was called the Gymnasium. The idea was to leave all the gym equipment for the guests to play on. The E.P.I. played there and tried to resuscitate the atmosphere they had created the previous April at the Dom, but they couldn't get an exclusive lease on the place and the location was poor.

CHRIS STEIN: Everything picked up when Sgt. Pepper came out in 1967. I used to play out in Brooklyn with my friends' bands. It was an ongoing thing, it wasn't career-oriented, it was just communication. Everybody was always on the periphery of the art scene and I had this friend who was a cute little boy with super long blond hair who was a gofor for Andy at the Factory. One night he said, "Listen, I can get you guys a gig opening for The Velvet Underground at the Gymnasium." I had never seen The Velvet Underground but we had the Banana album and everybody knew who they were, so we said, "Oh fantastic!" The night of the gig we got on the subway with our instruments and we were totally hippied out. We had balloons and a couple of girlfriends and everybody was dressed in beads and feathers. It was like a be-in on the subway floating towards Manhattan. We were ready to go, although we had previously only played in the living room or the basement.

It was pretty late at night by the time we got out of the subway in Manhattan and headed toward the Gymnasium. Walking down the block with our guitars we actually saw some people coming down the street and they said, "Oh, are you guys the band, because we've been waiting there all night and we wouldn't take it any more, we left because they never showed up." So we said, "Yeah, we're the band." We went inside and there was hardly anyone there. Somebody said Andy was supposed to be there, but he was off in the shadows with his entourage, we never saw him. We hung around for a little while and they played records, then we headed up for the stage. It was a big echoey place, we had absolutely no conception of playing a place like this whatsoever, but Maureen Tucker said we could use their equipment. So we plugged into their amps and the amps were all cranked up superloud. All Maureen had was a bass drum and a snare drum, but they were both turned on their side so the drummer was completely thrown off, but she said, "Well, it's OK, you can put them right side up," and somehow they produced a bass pedal from somewhere. Then we tried to play, but we were totally floored because we couldn't play in this huge resounding echo. It was a giant gymnasium with basketball hoops and everything was echoing so we couldn't really handle that, but we hacked our way through our little blues songs and people sort of watched us at first and then some of them tried to dance. The only song I remember doing was You Can't Judge A Book By Its Cover. We must have done a few more, but I remember sitting down after a while because the whole thing had gotten me pretty discouraged. Then somebody came over and said, "Oh Andy likes you, he thinks you're great." We must have played five or six songs then we just gave up. By that time the rest of the Velvets had arrived. After a while they started to play and they were like awesomely powerful. I had never expected to experience anything like that before. They just completely filled up the whole room with their sound. They were really into this huge fucking volume, and it was completely awesome. I was really disappointed that they didn't have Nico, because we thought she was the lead singer, but I distinctly remember the violin and their doing Venus In Furs because a couple of people in dark outfits got up and started doing a slow dance with a chain in between them. They did practically all the stuff from the Banana album. There were maybe 30 people there. It was very late, but it was a memorable experience. It was the dominant confident power of the whole thing that stayed with me.

BOCKRIS: Is it true that John Cale's father is deaf and his mother is mute?

BETSEY JOHNSON: No! His father's got a coal-miner's sense of humour. They don't talk in Wales, they sing. He was very very funny and their whole thing was watching Tom and Jerry. They had no cars on the street in Cumminford. We were there the Christmas of '67. We lived together a year before we got married.

BOCKRIS: When did you first become aware of The Velvet Underground?

JOHNSON: When they asked me to do clothes. That must have been the linkage. That's when I fell in love with John. Lou and I don't and never did sync. It's in the stars, because underneath John is an old-fashioned romantic who wants to come home

58

and have the wife with apron, kiss and hello, scratch his back and get his slippers and pipe. After going to Wales I really understood what he was all about. The first real time I talked with the Velvets was on a work-collaboration. I figured that's when we really had something to say to each other. Lou wanted grey suede. For Sterling and Maureen I did dark green and maroony velvets with all the little nail-head studs. But John wanted his hand to be on fire while he played. And he wanted to wear a mask. I think he wore masks a couple of times. I never did masks for him but I think he had them in black. I remember them a lot in Philadelphia and Boston. I thought that they were great. I mean, they were our band. I fell in love with John and we started living together when we were both in the Hotel Chelsea. Janis Joplin was there. Later I got a loft on La Guardia Place, and we were there for a while, and then we just decided to get married. The awful thing was The Ladies' Home Journal, the Magazine of Togetherness, was very much interested in us freaks then. I must have established some kind of something for myself at Paraphernalia, the press was really great. Ladies' Home Journal found out we were getting married and was going to pay for this huge bash. They just wanted to be there and photograph the freaky little rock'n'roll scene wedding ceremony and party even though we did it at City Hall. It was all set up and we had all the wedding invitations printed and they were all set to go to the mail box and the day that they were supposed to go in the mail John was turning bright yellow! He went to the hospital and I said, "Well, dear, when shall I mail these out? I'll wait for you to get your blood test." He didn't even leave the hospital. He went straight into quarantine with hepatitis and a non-existent liver. He was in the hospital for four months. Then the doctors took a sample and he walked out with a perfect liver. They could not believe it! They were afraid he was going to kick over, he was so saffron. Ladies' Home Journal was so outraged that they wanted me to go on with the whole wedding, go to City Hall, no John, and then they said, "Well, later we'll take a picture of John and strip him in!" Lou wasn't very happy John was getting married period, to me period. Because it was like two guys wanting to be stars. They were the perfect match, but they were the perfect mismatch in that their true-deep-down directional head for music was very different and I think John really respected Lou's more commercial kind of ability. That was when the group was together because Lou was just . . . it was like the girl breaking up the group.

BOCKRIS: What sort of financial state were they in at this point?

JOHNSON: Well, I don't remember chipping in. I loved John. I loved his work. I loved the group's craziness. I had a place. I was making money. He didn't have to worry about rent or food.

BOCKRIS: It's hard to know from this perspective to what extent the Velvets recognized their talent and lived the lifestyle to the full.

JOHNSON: They never did. In the '60s, none of us did.

BOCKRIS: It was always very uncertain?

JOHNSON: The Velvets were totally insecure all the time I think. I worried that John was going to be alive every day, even though I didn't want to know at all about what he was doing to himself. It was an on-the-edge kind of time every day. That was the great side of it.

BOCKRIS: Was this vulnerability like, in a sense, a very strong paranoia or just sheer fragility of the creative being on the edge the whole time?

JOHNSON: All of it. I never took a drug in the '60s. I wanted to smoke grass but John could never smoke grass, so I never got introduced.

BOCKRIS: Why not?

JOHNSON: He'd get paranoid craziness. So I didn't even go near. I thought he was real special because of that, that craziness to me was incredibly interesting. But especially after I moved away, too. He was really the kind that would be afraid to go out into the street from paranoia or whatever makes you that way. I don't think any of us were too secure outside of our little realm. I always felt very out of it because I was in a commercial business with a price-tag. I felt, they're the creative people, I'm the commercial kind of thing. I had the kind of schedule to keep to.

BOCKRIS: Did you get the sense that The Velvet Underground was John's whole life?

JOHNSON: Yeah! But then I remember Terry Riley being around a lot, and La Monte Young. Nico used to come over and live under my big stainless steel sink. And the whole loft was just music. We had a little bed in the corner.

BOCKRIS: Did you see John's personality breaking in two, in the sense that on the one hand he was a very creative personality balancing on the edge, on the other hand he had a very old-fashioned romantic sensibility?

JOHNSON: Yeah . . . and on the other hand he always wanted that hit 45 or hit single. He's the same way now.

FINKELSTEIN: I could never figure out whether John Cale wanted to be Elvis Presley, the Frankenstein monster, or young Chopin.

THE VELVET UNDERGROUND AND NICO LP

CALE: We were trying to do a Phil Spector thing with as few instruments as possible. On some tracks it worked. Venus In Furs is the best, and All Tomorrow's Parties and Sunday Morning. The band never again had as good a producer as Tom Wilson. He did those songs, plus Heroin and Waiting For The Man. They were done in LA at Cameo-Parkway. Andy Warhol (*credited prominently as producer*) didn't do anything; the rest were done by a businessman who came up with $1,500 for us to go into a broken-down studio and record the thing. I wasn't writing songs until Lou and I did Little Sister for Nico's Chelsea Girls LP. Whenever Lou and I worked together, I'd play piano and he would flip whatever version he had around it. I didn't contribute lyrics to any of his songs; he contributed to some of mine. We collaborated slightly on Sunday Morning, Black Angel's Death Song and, later, Lady Godiva's Operation. Most of it would be written, but a small part would be unresolved and Lou would resolve it.

61

SIDE ONE:

• Sunday Morning was originally composed by Lou Reed and John Cale sitting at a piano together in a friend's apartment at 6am one Sunday morning after being out all night (according to Lynne Tillman who was going out with Cale at the time).

• Waiting For The Man is about scoring heroin in Harlem.

• Femme Fatale was written for Nico, with Andy's encouragement by Lou, partially in collaboration with Sterling Morrison.

REED: We wrote Femme Fatale about somebody who was one, and has since been committed to an institution for being one. And will one day open up a school to train others.

• Venus In Furs –

REED: The prosaic truth is that I'd just read a book with this title by Leopold Sacher-Masoch and I thought it would make a great song title so I had to write a song to go with it. But it's not necessarily what I'm into.

MORRISON: We do love songs of every description. Venus In Furs is just a different kind of love song (Malanga knelt on stage and kissed Mary Woronov's black leather boots during this song). Everybody was saying this is the vision of all-time evil and I always said, "Well, we're not going to lie. It's pretty. Venus In Furs is a beautiful song. It was the closest we ever came in my mind to being exactly what I thought we could be. Always on the other songs I'm hearing what I'm hearing, but I'm also hearing what I wish I were hearing."

• Run Run Run is about Union Square, a notorious drug park, between 14th and 17th Streets in downtown Manhattan.

• All Tomorrow's Parties, Andy Warhol's all-time favourite Velvets' song was also written by Lou for Nico.

SIDE TWO:

• Heroin –

MORRISON: Heroin is a beautiful song too, possibly Reed's greatest and a truthful one. It's easy to rationalize about a song you like, but it should be pointed out that when Reed sings he's only glamorizing heroin for people who want to die. The real damage, particularly in New York, has been done through the cult of personality. Rock fans have taken heroin thinking Lou took heroin, forgetting that the character in the song wasn't necessarily Lou Reed.

REED: I'm not advocating anything. It all happened quite simply at the start. It's just that we had Heroin, Waiting For The Man, and Venus In Furs all on the first album, and that just about set the tone. It's like we also had Sunday Morning which was so pretty and I'll Be Your Mirror, but everyone psyched into the other stuff.

• There She Goes Again is a tough song about a tough chick.

• I'll Be Your Mirror: Lou must have been in love with Nico when he wrote this beautiful, tender love song.

• The Black Angel's Death Song was a precursor in a number of different veins.

MORRISON: A good friend of ours who saw many shows (and even played bass in one at the Dom) Helen Byrne ran up to me after the release of the album and exclaimed, "The Black Angel's Death Song – it's got chords!" Apparently she hadn't noticed in the live performances. "Of course, it's got chords!" I replied. "It's a song, isn't it?"

• European Son: Dedicated to Delmore Schwartz (who hated rock lyrics intensely, which is why the piece employed the fewest words on the album) simply because they wanted to dedicate something to him. John Cale ran a chair into some metal plates which scatter and sound like broken glass on this track.

MORRISON: European Son is very tame now. It happens to be melodic and if anyone actually listens to it, European Son turns out to be comprehensible in the light of all that has come since – not just our work but everyone's. It's that just for the time it was done it's amazing.

We figured that on our first album it was a novel idea just to have long tracks. People just weren't doing that – regardless of what the content of the track was – everyone's album cuts had to be 2.30 or 2.45. Then here's European Son which ran nearly eight minutes. All the songs on the first album are longish compared to the standards of the time.

CRAZY DIAMOND

Syd Barrett & The Dawn Of Pink Floyd

MIKE WATKINSON & PETE ANDERSON

**Syd Barrett was the erratically brilliant core of
Pink Floyd, then an acclaimed solo artist. When he
quit the music business, it was, amazingly, for ever.
Most people who reach the kind of cult status
occupied by Barrett do so by dying, but Syd lives on.
Watkinson and Anderson's book follows him through
his long exile from the public gaze. In this chapter,
set in the mid-'70s, Syd is at a low personal ebb while
Pink Floyd, without him, have become one of the
biggest groups on earth. Unexpectedly, their paths
cross for the last time . . .**

IRONICALLY, DURING THIS period of inactivity, Barrett's personal
income began to grow. The arrival of a fat royalties cheque for
the Floyd compilation album Relics – released in May 1971 –
allowed him to stay briefly on the top floor of London's Hilton
Hotel. David Bowie's version of See Emily Play on his 1973
album Pin-Ups coupled with the re-packaging of Floyd's first
two albums as A Nice Pair, in December 1973, also served to
increase his wealth.

Bowie was a Floyd fan during the UFO days but in a 1973
interview he said that after Syd left, "For me, there was no
more Pink Floyd." His controversial version of Barrett's best
known song drew a varied response from the critics. Ian
McDonald of New Musical Express felt Bowie had ruined the
song but Andrew Wood of International Times declared it the
best track on the album, saying: "It screams of Syd Barrett."

Kevin Ayers had already included a more personal Barrett tribute on his Bananamour album. The song Oh, Wot A Dream was about, and dedicated to, Syd and briefly available as a single. Ayers commented: "The sincerest form of flattery being imitation, it's quite deliberately sung in Syd Barrett's style. What I tried to do was get some of the feeling that's unique to him, just to show him that although we don't talk or meet, I have a certain closeness to what he's doing and can relate to it."

Once more the unwitting object of public attention, Barrett moved back to London in search of a new flat. He was bored with Cambridge and somewhat irritated by the steady stream of callers to his door. The prospect of anonymity in the big city was very appealing.

Syd plumped for a large two-bedroom flat at the exclusive Chelsea Cloisters apartment block, just off the King's Road. While the legend around him continued to grow out of all proportion to his recorded output, he spent his days sprawled in front of a huge bubble-shaped television set which hung from the ceiling. Over the previous two years, various sources had claimed that he was 1) working part-time in a factory; 2) had tried to enrol as an architectural student; 3) was growing mushrooms in a basement; 4) was living the life of a tramp; 5) had spent two weeks busking in New York, and 6) had tried to become a Pink Floyd roadie.

The mystique surrounding Barrett led in late 1972 to the formation of The Syd Barrett International Appreciation Society which produced a magazine called Terrapin and had area secretaries in Britain, Canada and the United States. The society clearly had Barrett's best interests at heart, though Nick Kent of NME acidly described it "as trivial as it is fanatical", and Barrett never even acknowledged its existence. The society's raison d'être was to encourage Syd to go back into the recording studio. It folded in mid-1974 amid a series of internal squabbles which were gleefully reported by the music press. Undaunted, Bernard White, a former area secretary, formed a new society which continued to publish Terrapin much to the chagrin of his former associates. White, a self-styled world authority on Barrett, continues to put out the occasional edition of Terrapin to this day.

Barrett's cult status was neatly captured in an excellent NME article by Nick Kent in the spring of 1974. Kent, who professed to being obsessed by Barrett himself, told readers that such notables as Jimmy Page, Brian Eno and Kevin Ayers had long wanted to work with the man whose only regular contact with the outside world consisted of sporadic visits to his publisher's office near Berkeley Square whenever the rent was due.

Kent wrote: "On one of his last visits, Bryan Morrison started getting insistent that Barrett write some songs. After all, demand for new Syd Barrett material is remarkably high at the moment and EMI are all set to swoop the lad, producer in tow, into the studio at any given moment. Barrett claimed that, no, he hadn't written anything but dutifully agreed to get down and produce some sort of something. His next appearance at the office occurred last week. Asked if he had written any new tunes, he replied in his usual hazy condition, hair somewhat grown out from its former scalp-shaved condition, 'No.' He then promptly disappeared again."

Morrison was strong-willed and used to getting his own way. His limited supply of patience was rapidly running out and what little remained vanished a few months later when Syd literally bit the hand that fed him. Barrett allegedly turned up at the office asking for his monthly royalty cheque. Morrison refused, claiming Syd had received it a week earlier. After several minutes haggling, the enraged Barrett vaulted over his manager's desk and bit the end of Morrison's little finger. According to singer Roy Harper, Syd actually bit off the end of Morrison's finger tip, and far-fetched as the tale sounds, it might explain why Morrison, even today, is uncharacteristically reticent on the subject of Syd.

Kent described Barrett's story as "a huge tragedy shot through with so many ludicrously comic aspects" and claimed to have heard literally hundreds of Syd yarns during the course of his investigations. Only recently, he reported, the Madcap had visited a King's Road boutique where he tried on three vastly different sizes of the same style of trousers, professed that they all fitted perfectly, then vanished without buying any of them.

The NME article, and a growing awareness of a revival of interest in Syd, prompted EMI to release his two albums in a double package that summer. Storm Thorgeson suggested a rather moving cover concept showing dozens of Barrett photographs and newspaper cuttings arranged like a fan's shrine to a departed hero. EMI, however, insisted on a current photo of the fallen hero, in self-imposed exile within Chelsea Cloisters. Thorgeson was dispatched on the difficult mission of photographing the unstable friend he'd not seen for years. Finding Syd was relatively easy, it was only when Thorgeson arrived at flat 902 on the ninth floor of Chelsea Cloisters that the tricky part came. Syd's response was a terse: "Go away. I don't want a photo." With that he slammed the door shut.

Thorgeson: "He was of course quite within his rights to resist intrusion if he didn't want it. But I got the impression he was just being fucking difficult and that really upset me."

A couple of months later, in November 1974, Jenner fared little better when he managed to coax Syd into the studio. Any lingering hope of a fruitful session disappeared when Syd arrived with a stringless guitar. A set of strings was eventually procured from Phil May of The Pretty Things but Floyd biographer Miles described how the proceedings degenerated into grim charade: "When everything seemed in order they began. Syd had asked someone to type his lyrics to his new songs for him. This they had done using the red ribbon of the typewriter. When the sheet was handed to Syd he thought it was a bill, grabbed the guy's hand and tried to bite his fingers off. Syd was in the studio for three days. The material put down on tape was described as 'extremely weird' and had a 'strong hardly-begun feel to it'. Only the backing tracks were recorded, no vocal tracks at all, and there is some doubt as to whether Syd even bothered to turn up on the third day. The material never reached the stage where it could be mixed and consequently remains unissued."

Jenner sees the sessions as a painful exercise in futility. He had tried to play the understanding liberal but Barrett was unhappy even under Jenner's relaxed command and he frequently disappeared for brooding walks around the studio. Jenner: "The engineer used to say that if he turned right he'd be back but if he went left he'd be gone for the day. He was never wrong."

The whole experience renewed Barrett's recurring fear of the limelight. On one of his unending walks around London he was spotted by Bernard White. Thrilled at the prospect of a pavement chat with his idol, White pursued the fleeing Barrett down Regent Street until a plaintive "Please go away" stopped him in his tracks. Crestfallen, White, who had dedicated his adult life to collecting Barrett memorabilia, watched the Madcap disappear among the afternoon shoppers.

White's chance encounter was duly logged in Terrapin's regular "Syd Sightings" column. The original Barrett Appreciation Society attributed its closure to 'a lack of Syd' and it is ironic to consider that the fanaticism of Barrett's most loyal supporters may unintentionally have contributed to his withdrawal.

Around the same time, one of Syd's old Cambridge friends was driving along Oxford Street when he suddenly spied him loping along the pavement. Braking to a halt, the friend leapt out and scurried after the retreating figure of Syd who stonily ignored his greeting. His forward gaze did not falter, nor did he slow down. Finally the perplexed friend asked Syd where he was walking to. Barrett stopped, turned, and fixed his piercing green eyes on the pursuer. "Far further than you could possibly imagine," he said before striding off purposefully.

Chelsea Cloisters provided a welcome retreat for Syd. The impressive red-brick apartment block is situated in the quiet Chelsea hinterland, only five minutes walk from the King's Road. Its exclusive clientèle enjoy a first-class service from staff who never intrude on their privacy. One of the porters, Ronnie Salmon, witnessed Syd's bizarre behaviour over eight years.

Shortly after he started work there in January 1974, one of his colleagues identified the reclusive character on the ninth floor as "Syd Barrett, the guy who used to be in Pink Floyd."

Salmon first met Barrett when he was summoned to flat 902 to remove the huge oval television that had dominated the living room and, until this moment, most of its occupant's time. Syd took him along to a sixth-floor storeroom where he kept five or six guitars, numerous amps and a box containing several tapes. Barrett collected the guitars and told the startled porter he could have all that was left – tapes, amps, records and two portable televisions.

According to Salmon, the box, possibly containing tapes of the recent studio sessions, disappeared when he popped into an Oxford Street store. The hapless porter put the box down to try on some new clothes, then walked out without it. Realising his error, he hurried back to the store only to find that the box had vanished along with some of Syd's best kept secrets.

Salmon: "When I first came to know him, he was slim with long hair and the colourful clothes he wore could have come straight off their first album cover. Once he called me up to his flat and showed me a Dynatron remote control television in a beautiful cabinet. He gave it to me. He said he didn't want it."

Just as buying endless guitars had been an expensive luxury a couple of years earlier, Syd was now fascinated with televisions and had half-a-dozen in his flat at one point. But he had never cared much for money or the material wealth that went with it. His attachment to personal belongings had always been transitory, and he quickly grew bored with any new "toy". As early as Floyd's 1967 American tour, he bought a pink Cadillac in San Francisco – and gave it away a few days later to someone he met in the street. Green with envy, Salmon's fellow porters watched with growing disbelief at the endless stream of freebies he brought down from flat 902. "The other guys couldn't work it out but Mr Barrett seemed to like me and talked to me the most."

Salmon's theory later proved unfounded when Syd began handing out giveaways to all and sundry. One porter received some hi-fi equipment and a third got yet another discarded television. When a delivery man brought round a state-of-the-art Dynatron sound system, he was given a £300 tip and told to share it with his friends.

Salmon: "He used to buy things and then throw them away. He gave his guitars away to friends – really beautiful Fender Stratocasters. One day he walked out of the foyer with a Harrods bag and I followed him down Sloane Avenue. He threw it in a dustbin and I was curious to see what it was. It turned out to be a brand new clock radio worth £100. He used to buy suits and shirts one day and throw them away the next. He was a nice guy and usually seemed in a happy frame of mind. He had a fair bit of mail and quite a few visitors including people from the music business."

Even in this relatively tranquil period, the darker side of Syd's nature occasionally broke through. Salmon: "Once he smashed the door of his flat off its hinges. I think he was 'high' a lot of the time. His mind was there – and yet it wasn't."

Syd's eccentricity also surfaced from time to time such as when he appeared before Salmon in the foyer wearing a dress, his head newly shaven.

"He had on a Crombie coat with a dress underneath and a pair of plimsolls. I ran after him because I couldn't believe what I'd seen, and there he was walking down Sloane Avenue." Syd had brought Arnold Layne to life and the disarming display no doubt appealed to his creator's dark sense of humour.

Back in the real world, Peter Jenner was suffering pangs of guilt about Syd's demise but publicly declared his continued faith in him. He told a Canadian radio interviewer that Syd's talent was still there but his songs were sketches rather than paintings: "He's a great artist, an incredibly creative artist and it's tragic that the music business may well have a lot to do with doing him in. I think we have a lot to answer for – myself and everyone else involved with him."

During this period, Syd decided on a change of image. One day he stunned Chelsea Cloisters staff by arriving down in the foyer without any hair. When it grew back he took to cutting and bleaching it himself.

Salmon: "He used to drink in The Marlborough (public house) just round the corner and went from slim to fat. He became really bloated within a matter of months because he was drinking Guinness all the time. When I used to go round for a few beers with my mates, we'd see him sitting over in the corner as if in a dream. He was on his own all the time . . . always on his own. I'd try and get him to talk about his music but he just wasn't interested."

Although Syd showed no interest in his own music, he had a celebrated reunion with Pink Floyd at Abbey Road during the 1975 sessions for the Wish You Were Here album. Those close to the Floyd believed the band were dangerously close to splitting up. Worn out by an endless series of tours and recording sessions, their efforts to produce a successor to the phenomenally successful Dark Side Of The Moon album were becoming increasingly tortuous. Gilmour insists that the album itself was not dedicated to Barrett but its opening track and key song Shine On You Crazy Diamond is clearly a thinly-veiled tribute. It was developed from the mournful guitar motif played by Gilmour at the start of the 26-minute piece. Gilmour: "I found it by accident but it stirred something in me and I kept playing it. It obviously worked because Roger said: 'Hey, what's that you're playing?'"

Midway through the album, the band heard a strange rumour that Syd had been spotted outside Harrods wearing a large Yogi Bear tie. They didn't pay much attention as such Barrett tales were by now commonplace. They were, therefore, quite unprepared for the events of June 5 when Gilmour noticed a shaven-headed, overweight figure walking rather absent-mindedly around Studio 3 at Abbey Road: "This guy was walking around looking at the equipment. At first I didn't take much notice because I thought it was one of EMI's staff boffins. Then later he came into the control room. He was there for a long time and we were all whispering: 'Who the fuck's this funny geezer?' I think I was the first to recognise him."

Storm Thorgeson, who arrived for Gilmour's wedding reception later that same day, recalls Syd wearing a white mackintosh with white shoes and carrying a white bag. "Two or three people cried. He sat round and talked for a bit but he wasn't really there."

Andrew King, one of the invited wedding guests, thought Barrett looked like "the type of bloke who serves you in a hamburger bar in Kansas City." He adds: "He was fat and his hair was thinning on top. He was wearing a very short-sleeved sports shirt and American-type slacks. The Floyd took it very badly. What could they say? But everyone else had their problems and they knew Syd still had a good income."

Jerry Shirley was equally shocked when he attended the wedding banquet in the EMI canteen that afternoon:

"Sitting opposite me was this hulk with a bald head. He must have weighed about 15 stone. While I was eating, this guy was looking at me rather strangely and smiling. I thought he was a Hare Krishna freak until Dave, who was sitting a few places down on the other side, saw I was unnerved and motioned me over. I went round and he said: 'Do you know who that is?' Just as he said that I was looking at the guy from the side and something about his profile made me realise it was Syd. I went over and asked him how things were going. He was chuckling over the fact that I hadn't recognised him. Syd spent the rest of the meal looking at my wife in a disconcerting manner and I think he disappeared as mysteriously as he had arrived."

None of the Floyd have seen Syd from that day to this, but a month later, their headlining festival appearance in the grounds of the stately home at Knebworth, Hertfordshire, was the setting for another strange incident. The band's first set was a complete rendition of the songs on Wish You Were Here. Roy Harper sang on Have A Cigar just as he did on the album version. According to Harper, who was also managed by Blackhill, a set of photographs were taken earlier in the day when Floyd-versus-Blackhill cricket match was held in the festival grounds.

Harper: "When the snaps were passed round at Abbey Road a week later, somebody said: 'My God, that's Syd!' We all crowded round to have a look and I'm absolutely certain it was Syd. There was this bald overweight figure actually standing next to me in one of the photos yet no one could remember seeing him there at the time."

The tale is brusquely dismissed by Gilmour as: "Just another of those stupid stories. The idea of Syd being this spectre hanging over us is complete shit." Even so, the story comes from a number of different sources and Syd wouldn't have found it that difficult to reach Knebworth from London. Considering his physical appearance, the fact no one recognised him is not too surprising. He was the subject of at least one of the songs in the Floyd's set so it would be natural for him to want to see its first public performance. When Roger Waters had played Shine On to him at Abbey Road, Syd had reportedly said it sounded "a bit old".

Waters explained how the song evolved: "It was very strange. I don't know why I started writing those lyrics about Syd. I think because that phrase of Dave's was an extremely mournful kind of sound, but it was a long time before the Wish You Were Here recording sessions when Syd's state could be seen as symbolic of the general state of the group, that is very fragmented.

"I'm very sad about Syd. Of course he was important and the band would never have fucking started without him because he was writing all the material. It couldn't have happened without him but on the other hand it couldn't have gone on with him. Shine On is not really about Syd – he's just a symbol for all the extremes of absence some people have to indulge in because it's the only way they can cope with how fucking sad it is, modern life, to withdraw completely. I found that terribly sad."

1976 is remembered as the year of the punk rock explosion and the overthrow of traditional heroes and values. A decade after the apogee of Swinging London, it was regarded as a sin to profess a liking for The Beatles or the Stones – a crime that

Malcolm McLaren used as an excuse to sack Glen Matlock from the Sex Pistols. Although Johnny Rotten strutted down the King's Road in an "I hate Pink Floyd" T-shirt, Syd himself was far from an object of derision.

Early that year, the Pistols' art director Jamie Reid contacted Barrett expert Bernard White about the possibility of Syd producing the group's first album. The Pistols' Machiavellian manager Malcolm McLaren was a big Barrett fan. White, of course, was unable to contact Syd, still resolutely locked away in his high-class fortress, and The Pistols were similarly unsuccessful during a brief but tumultuous stay at Chelsea Cloisters. When the band's infamy is taken into account, Syd's reluctance to open his door to McLaren's spiky-haired mob is perhaps not surprising.

While Syd proved an elusive quarry for the Pistols, he developed a habit of haunting old friends and acquaintances when least expected. Producer Malcolm Jones met Barrett outside the HMV store and Jack Monck exchanged a brief greeting with him in Charing Cross Road. On a trip to Harrods, Twink was standing on the up escalator and was startled to see Barrett pass by silently on the one going down. On another occasion, Syd burst into Jenner and King's Blackhill office in Bayswater as if such an appearance warranted not a hint of surprise. Although they were no longer handling his affairs, Syd asked for, and was given, his passport. No one asked, or was told, why he wanted it.

Syd's heavyweight look made these occasional sightings all the more shocking. No one could quite believe how the once-skeletal Barrett frame had transformed so dramatically in such a short space of time. Capital Radio DJ Nicky Horne attempted to interview Syd and later told the News Of The World:

"I knocked on the door and this huge fat man answered wearing only pyjama trousers. He'd shaved off his eyebrows and looked incredibly strange. I thought he was a minder. He looked down at me and said, 'Syd can't talk.' When I told Dave Gilmour he said the man had been Syd and he'd been telling the truth. He really couldn't talk any more."

Bernard White: "When I saw a photo of Syd taken at the Wish You Were Here sessions I just had to sit down. I'd bumped into him only nine months before that and the change was unbelievable."

Syd's growing fondness for Guinness, coupled with boredom and a royalties income that enabled him to dine out at the more expensive London restaurants, were the chief causes of his expanding waistline.

In the summer of 1977, ex-fiancée Gayla Pinion was shopping in South Kensington when she turned and saw Syd: "He stood there juggling a tin of Campbell's soup in one hand and just laughing at me. He must have been a good stone heavier and his hair was cut in a short back and sides." Syd's appearance reminded Gayla of his far-fetched idea of pursuing a medical career. "Standing there in his white shirt and pin-striped suit, he looked just like a doctor." Slightly unnerved and unable to believe this was the man she had nearly married, Gayla prepared to leave the store: "When we got outside I couldn't resist any longer and called after him. He swung round and just said, 'Fancy seeing you here'."

Gayla was surprised when Syd invited her to a pub as he had never drunk much when she was with him. Over a half-pint of cider and the inevitable pint of Guinness, he invited her back to Chelsea Cloisters and a cautious Gayla accepted the offer. "When we got there I found all the curtains were drawn, no windows were open and there was this horrible smell. In the middle of the room was a huge television." It brought back too many painful memories and declining a cup of tea, Gayla nipped out of the door while Syd pottered about in the kitchen.

The following spring, New York freelance writer Kris DiLorenzo produced an article for Trouser Press magazine, undoubtedly the best since Nick Kent's thoughtful study in 1974. Jerry Shirley expressed doubts over whether Syd would ever record again – "He would have to return to this planet long enough for someone to believe that he's got it in him to actually get to the sessions" – and Bryan Morrison cleared up a few mysteries: "He doesn't have any involvement with anything or anybody. He is a recluse with about 25 guitars around him. I see him very rarely. I mean, I know where he is, but he doesn't want to be bothered; he just sits there on his own watching TV all day and getting fat. That's what he does."

Asked whether anyone could talk Syd into recording again, Morrison's negative response merely confirmed Shirley's gloomy forecast: "No, it's impossible."

Barrett was firmly anchored in his shell but this did nothing to deter pioneering punk band The Damned from attempting to persuade Syd to produce their second album later that year. Captain Sensible and the rest of the band were Barrett freaks who hoped the Madcap's presence would give the album an eccentric slant and early Floyd influence. Captain Sensible: "During rehearsals we discovered we all loved the early Floyd stuff so we approached some people who knew Syd but they said it wasn't really on. In the end we had to make do with Nick Mason and he didn't have a clue." In her biography The Book Of The Damned Carol Clerk described Music For Pleasure as a "dismal desperate record" and quoted the band saying Mason was not the man for the job. "He just didn't know the band, didn't understand the energy that we had before. Also the songs weren't really there and he didn't give us any guidance in that. We were trying to get into his world and he was trying to get into ours and the two never met. There was a hell of a lot of disillusionment."

Floyd had long since come to accept that even a decade after the split they would never be free of Barrett's influence. Questions on Barrett were an obligatory part of every interview. Rick Wright was quizzed about his former colleague in an interview on Montreal Radio's The Pringle Show in December 1978. "He (Syd) is probably like he has been for the past seven years. He's very weird. I haven't seen him for years. The last time I saw him was when we did Wish You Were Here and he just turned up. I don't know what he's like in his head because he does not talk at all. It's very sad. He can't relate to anyone. He's not a vegetable; his brain's ticking away, but just somewhere else completely. He literally is on another planet."

Wright was asked whether he thought drugs had contributed to Syd's decline: "The drugs don't cause these things. Drugs are just a catalyst if you like. It has to be in your brain first of all – for example, some people can take acid every day of their life and come out of it all right. I know he took the whole lot at this period of time but if he hadn't taken it, I still think he would have gone the way he has. But you never know. (Syd) did get more and more into a group of people who were acidheads which we tried to stop because we could see it was going to destroy him. They won and we lost."

Roger Waters, who felt Barrett's influence on the latter-day Floyd was grossly exaggerated, was driven to exasperation by the incessant probing of interviewers. In a 1976 interview with Street Life, which first appeared in the French monthly Rock Et Folk, he was reminded that he had recently described Syd as "slobbish, empty and incapable of creativity".

Waters: "Really? My violent reaction is explained by getting snowed under with gossips and snippets that each and everybody put out about Syd. These wouldn't have been brought up if Syd had had some success. Or if we hadn't had any ourselves. For my part I've never read an intelligent piece about Syd Barrett in any magazine. Never. No one knows what they are talking about. Only us, the people who knew him and who still know him a bit. Only we know the facts, how he lived, what happened to him, why he was doing certain things. They make me laugh all these journalists and their rubbish. In actual fact I wrote that song Shine On above all to see the reactions of those people who reckon they know and understand Syd Barrett. There's a feeling in that piece, I don't know, that sort of indefinable, inevitable melancholy about the disappearance of Syd . . . because he's left, withdrawn so far away that, as far as we're concerned, he's no longer there."

The years of frivolous spending were coming to an end for Barrett. What had once seemed a bottomless pit of royalties ran dry and rising rents made it impossible for him to stay at Chelsea Cloisters. The following year, 1979, saw him back with his mother in Cambridge – a declared bankrupt.

Syd's return home coincided with a great wave of publicity for the release of Pink Floyd's album The Wall. Floyd took Another Brick In The Wall to the top of the singles charts and there was speculation that Syd had inspired some of Waters' surreal visions. When a New York DJ played the record backwards he located a secret message that many believed was a reference to Syd. "Congratulations," it began, "you have just discovered the secret message. Please send your answer to The Old Pink, care of The Funny Farm, Chalfont." Pink Floyd had no comment and it is more than likely that the message was added by some mischievous studio engineer or record pressing plant employee.

But as the subsequent film version of The Wall showed, there was an indisputable element of the Barrett saga in the story of the hero Pink, played by Bob Geldof, whose rise to stardom is accompanied by a descent into madness.

Gilmour: "The central character is based on all sorts of people. Syd was convenient for some of the stories. There was, for example, a swimming pool incident in Los Angeles. Syd fell in, took off his Granny Takes A Trip clothes, and left them lying by the poolside for three days." In the film Geldof cuts himself and, lying prostrate in a hotel pool, turns the water blood-red.

The album was an extraordinary commercial success. EMI shipped 600,000 sets in four weeks in the UK alone where it was retailing at £8.45 a copy. By the end of January, the figure was over 1,200,000 copies.

The gulf between Syd and his former band could scarcely have been wider. While the Floyd premièred The Wall at the Los Angeles Sports Arena, complete with inflatable pig, an animated film and crashing aeroplane, Barrett was once again ensconced in Cambridge, quietly living with his mother in another part of the city. Apart from a rumour that he turned up at the Abbey Road studio, guitar in hand and intent on resuming his recording career, only to be turned away when no one recognised him, little was heard of the Madcap in 1980.

The following year, a crop of new bands emerged whose

image and songwriting was based on '60s psychedelia. Many cited Barrett as a major influence including The Television Personalities, whose leader Dan Treacey penned a charming little song to someone he (wrongly) felt was in danger of becoming a forgotten hero. I Know Where Syd Barrett Lives sold several thousand copies, made the independent charts, and was even released in Japan under the misprinted title: I Know Where Syd Barrer Lives – the response of the fanatical Japanese record-buying public is unrecorded.

The band sent a copy of the record – an attempt at copying the Barrett style – to Syd's family who were quite touched. They were not so pleased with some of the dubious publicity the record brought in its wake. First off the mark was The Sun newspaper which told its credulous readers that a grotesquely overweight Syd was living in the attic of his mother's home and had taken advantage of one of his mother's shopping trips to nip downstairs and paint the fridge green before returning to his hiding place. Another man claimed to have met a vaguely familiar character enjoying a pint of Guinness in the King's Arms pub in Cambridge. When questioned about the superstar group he created, he replied: "Pink Floyd? I know the name… I think they owe me some money."

The stories were typical of the questionable Barrett tales that surfaced that summer. The "green fridge" episode is the stuff of which myths are made – an example of how wild rumour can come to be regarded as fact – and it has been faithfully recycled over the years, usually when one of the music papers puts out a "10 Rock Fruitcakes Of Our Time" list. With the passage of time it has become as much a part of Barrett folklore as the mandrax incident of 1967.

Reality was far more mundane. Syd's health left a lot to be desired. He had spent some time in a sanatorium in Essex but despite the undeniable benefits to his well-being, within weeks of returning home he was back in hospital to have a stomach ulcer removed. Feeling stronger by the summer of 1982 and having amassed a sizable sum in royalty back-payments, he once again took up residence at Chelsea Cloisters. His return was a pleasant surprise for porter Ronnie Salmon in more ways than one. The prospect of a healthy income from tips and handouts was restored but he was also amazed at the transformation in his former benefactor's appearance: "When he left here, he was as fat as a barrel and his head was shaved. Now here he was again – the original Syd Barrett looking just like he had in 1974. His hair had grown long and he was very thin. I said: 'Christ, you've lost a lot of weight' and he said he'd had a stomach ulcer."

The expected freebie bonanza never materialised: "He stayed here for a few weeks and then went back to Cambridge without even saying goodbye. We haven't seen him since."

ROCK LIVES

Timothy White

**Rock Lives is a huge compendium of interviews with
and profiles of the founding fathers of rock and pop,
the '60s and '70s giants who picked up the flame
from those pioneers, and the superstars of today.
The 60 or so subjects covered include Robert
Johnson, James Brown, Brian Wilson, Pete
Townshend, Elvis Costello and Prince. By affording
each generation and genre equal respect and
affection, White exposes and explores the threads of
motivation and experience shared by music people.
Reproduced here is a remarkable 1977 interview with
a 19-year-old Michael Jackson.
The Jacksons have just finished their Goin' Places
album, Michael has just completed The Wiz film
project with Diana Ross, Elvis Presley's
corpse is exactly a week old . . .**

Are you happy with the new Jacksons album, Goin' Places?

[Cautious, nodding] Umm hmm.

Your last album was the first one called The Jacksons, right? It got a lot of play in discos.

Yes. It did very well. They released a single *[Show You The Way To Go]* from that album in London, and it did very well. Went to Number 1. It was Number 1 for like two weeks in a row. And now they released Dreamer from that album. It's one of my favourite ones from that album. It's a ballad'n'all.

Goin' Places is supposed to be the single from the new album?

So far, they've chosen it.

Who chooses it? You?

Kenny Gamble, the producer, and the president of Columbia [*Walter Yetnikoff*].

Do you have any influence?

We talk to the guys and everything, you know, and tell them. Because they know we know what's good, and we know what the kids wanna hear. We dance, and we're out there all the time while they're in their offices. [*Grinning impishly*] So they know they better listen to what we say.

Are you hot for dance singles these days?

Yes. Both – ballads and dance singles. I just love to see the kids have a good time when the music come on. Sometime I sneak into this skating rink when they put them jams on. And you can tell when something's dirty: the kids be kicking in. Soon as there's something hot – *ow!* – they break out. Which is important, because people like to dance and have a good time.

Speaking of ballads, I think back to Ben. [Ben was written for the 1972 horror film Ben (the sequel to 1971's thriller about befriending rats, Willard) by composer Walter Scharf and lyricist Don Black. The recording session was co-produced by Freddie Perren, Fonce Mizell, Deke Edwards, and Berry Gordy, Jr. Michael Jackson had no credited role in creating the song.] Even though it was Number 1 in 1972, a lot of people don't know the song's about a rat. They haven't seen the film, so they see the song as a ballad about friendship.

Umm hmm. I like it both ways.

How do you mean?

I mainly like it as a record. I love rats. And I like it as a friend, too, as if I'm talking to a guy that's a friend of mine – [*blushing smile*] but none *other* than just a friend! Some people see it the rat way. Some people see it the friend way. It works both ways.

You're big on rats?

I *love* them. I used to raise them.

White rats? You raised them at home?

Yeah. In cages and things.

You've gotten out of it now?

[*Nodding*] You know, 'cause rats have weird characteristics. [*Very sheepishly*] They start eating one another. They really do.

It just got sickening to me, and I just said forget it. I came home one night and looked in the cage, and the rats had started eating each other. The *father* was eating the babies. I got sick of looking at it all and left their cage outside. I didn't realize how cold it was. The rats, still alive, froze to death. [*Laughs*] I don't mind talking about it, if you don't. Do you?

Plus, in Beverly Hills there's a lot of snakes. I almost got bit by one rattlesnake because of the rats. See, when you live up in the hills, that's what happens.

The rats draw snakes?

Umm hmm! Tremendously.

And it was cold enough in Beverly Hills one night to freeze the rats?

Yeah, oh yeah. See, it's high *up*. There was a strange mist around, a rainy type of coldness, and the snakes started coming out of the ground to get the rats. I guess I got caught in the middle of this thing. It was awful! [*Laughs*]

How many rats did you have?

Oh, I had quite a few. A lot of them. My mother hated it. I was up to about thirty rats.

Do they reproduce quickly?

[*Grimaces*] Weirdly quickly! You wake up one morning, and you see all these little things crawling around. It's fun, anyway.

Nobody clued you in on the rats' habit of eating each other?

Nope. I just saw it when they ate the babies. I shoulda separated the father from his children. I'd never see that deal. I had no idea, no idea. I don't think anybody knows the reason why – it doesn't exist; if they did say it, it's not a good enough reason.

Well, let's go back to the film. How were you approached to do the Scarecrow in The Wiz?

I was sitting at home one day, and the phone rings.

Home in Beverly Hills?

No, we don't live in Beverly Hills no more. We moved. See, we built this studio. And where we were staying we had a lot of room, but it wasn't enough. We always wanted to build a studio, 'cause we were rehearsing in our garage in Beverly

Hills and the neighbours complained. And so we moved to Encino, in the San Fernando Valley, got a lot more room now, and we built a studio in our house, and so now we record and do a lot more stuff in that house. That's what it's great for.

But anyway, getting back: I was sitting at home and the phone rings from our office, and they say, "Hey, Michael! How would you like to do The Wiz?" I said, "Well, where'd you get this news from?" He said, "Well, in New York City Rob Cohen and Sidney Lumet called." I said, "Yeah! I'd like to do it!"

The only reason why I said yes was because I knew a lot about the production and getting it together. And I knew it was some of the best people in the film industry working on this thing. Sidney Lumet is the hottest director of the time.

Had Diana stepped into the project at this time?

[Laughing] Oh yeah. I had called Diana up in Las Vegas, and she was telling me that she was gonna go to New York and film it, and I said, "Well I hope the best for you!" Next thing I know is I'm in the film!

So what sort of preparations have you made to play the Scarecrow? I assume you saw the old Wizard Of Oz movie?

Oh yeah, I have it on videotape. I watch it sometimes and just turn the sound down and watch the moves. When you see the old one, you realize – I had to say this – but you realize that they didn't bring out what they should have brought out. That's what The Wiz is all about – it's bringing out what Frank Baum, the writer, was really trying to say, in this movie. You can see where a lot was thrown out. We make it more recognizable to people what the story is all about.

Give me an example.

Well, the different characters, the Scarecrow with the brain thing. He *think* he doesn't have a brain, but he does. All the time it's there, but he don't *know* it. The whole thing is bringing it out.

What I do as the Scarecrow is, I don't think I'm smart and everything. And all through the movie I be bringing out these quotations from out of my sleeves'n'all. See, I'm *garbage* instead of straw; I'm filled with the stuff. And I'm reading these quotations from all over me about such and such: "Confucius said this." But I *still* think I'm ignorant.

So it will have a larger social impact than a whimsical kids' story?

[Solemnly] Umm hmm. It's a strong movie. Some people will see it as a kids' film, but it isn't. You can follow it as you go through your life. That's the main answers to life – with that whole movie. I mean you can just follow life with that movie. It's deeper than what people really think it is.

Have you read the original book?

[Embarrassed] I know I should. I was supposed to read it, but I haven't had the time.

If you do, you'll find it's not precisely a children's book. Diana Ross recently made the point that it never mentions how old Dorothy is.

Dorothy's not really in the story at all. Not that much. It's just the way MGM did it that makes people think she's a big part of it.

[Excited] You can find so many great things in The Wiz about life. There are so many smart people walking around that don't know they're smart, don't *believe* in themselves. It's helpful for that too.

That's what the Scarecrow is all about. He's a smart guy! There's these crows that come every day and jive me and say I'm dumb, I'm ignorant, I can't walk, I can't do this. And they're so cool they just walk into my garden and take advantage of me. I'm begging them, "Can't I get down just for one second and walk in the garden?" They say, "Man, you can't walk!"

One day my break comes when Dorothy helps me down. I've been reading all these quotes that show how smart I am, but I really don't know it. I know something's wrong with what they're telling me, but I can't put my finger on it, and something's still wrong.

It just brings out more. It's more of a city story. Instead of straw, it's garbage. The Tin Man is all kinda cans: peanut butter cans, and this and that. Toto is like a German shepherd puppy. It's really great; this is great!

It's a fantasy look, too. When I say we're gonna be on location, a lot of people think we're just gonna look real-to-life. With a sky like this one [*points out the window*]. No, we're gonna give it a real fantasy look. Some of the scenes will have 600 dancers! It's a $12 million production! That's how much they're spending.

What do you enjoy most about the filming?

[*Very softly*] I love the amazing make-up and all the costumes and all the excitement. And I love the dance sequences. We got some dance sequences gonna knock people down! [*Giggles*]

Are they working you too hard?

Not at all. It's just the opposite. I never want to stop. Sometimes I even come home in my make-up!

You're that attached to the character?

[*Nodding slowly*] It takes a long time to put it on my face, but I like how *different* it feels. I can be in a whole 'nother place with it. Sometime I wear it home, and people – kids – I look out the back window of the car and let them see me. Whoa, they get frightened! They don't know who or what it is! It's a trip, it's really a trip. [*Softly, guardedly*] It's a secret; that's it. I like that it's a secret.

[*Relaxing*] It's just a warm feeling inside, like I can do anything he does, and everybody will dig it. Because once he comes down from the pole in that corn patch, everybody appreciates the Scarecrow.

You've never done a film before, have you?

I've done so much acting but never in a film.

How do you mean?

Well, all the variety I've done, and different sketches on TV shows. I've done so much, you know, long sketches. I've done The Flip Wilson Show and Carol Burnett, all that stuff, Sonny and Cher. But I've never done a movie. This is the first one.

Are you scared?

No. Not at all, not at all. Honest to God, I'm not. I'm challenged. I love it. I'm not scared at all.

Even when I was very small, all I wanted to do was get into this performing kind of thing. But no matter how many movie offers come to me, music will always be my number one thing. Because it's inside of me, and it's something that has to come out. And it's still in there.

[Smiling shyly] Like when I'm going over my script, music just comes into my head, and songs, and I run to the tape recorder and put melodies on tape. *Constantly.* Not to wait for a piano for stuff, because I can't help it. I can't. I got to have it.

What was the first time you performed?

It was in a shopping centre, the Big Top, in Gary, Indiana. It was at a grand opening. All the people come around and buy the season fashions. We agreed to be in front of the mall, in the middle of it, and sing. And that's what we did.

You must have done some performing before that, to have that come about.

[Mulling] Yeah, but you know, I can't remember. I wasn't even thinking about that. I just *did* it. I was about six. I got started around five.

What is your earliest memory of performing? Did someone, your father maybe, take you by the hand and ask you to sing?

No, we were just singing around the house, old folk songs, Cotton Fields Back Home and *[sings]* Down In The Valley . . . We used to wake up singing.

We had bunk beds, and I would shack up with Marlon, and Tito would shack up with Jermaine, and Jackie would have his own on top. We would just sing every morning.

See, my father had a group, with his brothers, The Falcons. And Tito would sneak his guitar and play it when he'd go to work. When he got caught, Tito would get in so much trouble for playing Dad's guitar. One day Tito broke a string, and my father go so mad at Tito, he got so mad at him, so angry, he said, "Lemme see what you can play! If you can't play that, I'm a really *beat* you!"

Tito was scared, but when he *could* play, my father was shocked. He was so good, by just sneaking and playing. My father thought, Well, there's some kind of *talent* here, and he started saving up money, buying instruments and microphones and amplifiers.

We would do talent shows in the neighbourhood in Gary, and later at the high school. *[Proudly]* We would always win every one. We have all these trophies in our house, all over the place.

One day Gladys Knight told a guy named Bobby Taylor at Motown about us, and Motown got a hold of us. We did a show on Berry [Gordy]'s gigantic estate in Detroit, around the poolside. *All* the Motown stars were there: Diana Ross, The Temptations, everybody. They loved us, and we recorded our first record, I Want You Back, a three-million-seller. And we went on and on.

How old were you when you got the first hit?

On I Want You Back I was 10, but our very first one was a record [in 1968] called I'm A Big Boy Now on Steeltown, and it was a Gary, Indiana, company. It was a local hit.

Who wrote "Big Boy"?

[Frowning, shrugs] Boy, I don't know.

Do you remember how the song goes?

[Brightening, smiling] Yes. It's a good melody! It goes: *[sings]* "Fair-y tales, fair-y tales, have lost their charm. Da-da-da, da-da-da, a-da-da-da. 'Cause I'm a big boy now!" It's a good melody. It'd be a hit today, really. *[Insistent]* It could! You know, a lot of these people, they take these old songs and say the same thing, thinking, "The *kids* don't know it."

Sure, Rita Coolidge has a hit now with Higher And Higher.

That's right, that Jackie Wilson hit! People don't know, but they take those old songs and bring them back, and everybody think it's something new – when it's old. And I'm just listening to them and thinking, "My *mother* usta put on these records!"

So your father had a band called The Falcons, right? How much do you know about his band?

Well, it was his three brothers [the band had five members], and they were a little group from the South, with guitar, bass, and drums. Dad's from the South – Arkansas. I don't know what city.

Did he ever tell you any stories about the early days playing with The Falcons?

No. I don't think he needs to talk about it. We haven't talked about it. He's never talked about it. All we know is that he had a group. We know he was a good player, because they played in Gary when we were little. Then they were split up, but he would just grab his guitar and start playing . . .

. . . around the house?

Uh huh. And his brother played guitar very well, too. They would be jamming at the house, playing the blues and stuff. They all helped Tito learn how to play.

How many people in your dad's family, meaning brothers and sisters?

I think it was about four. I think there's three left.

Was your mom from Arkansas, too?

No. Alabama.

How did your dad meet your mom? Did they ever tell you?

[Shy giggle] They won't! Kitty starts blushing over the whole thing. I mention it, and she starts blushing. She says, "Now, why you wanna ask that?" I think it was in high school or something, when he was young.

You really don't know anything about how your parents met and courted?

[Softly] I don't know anything about it. They won't discuss it. [Giggles] It's hard to picture.

How do you get along with your father?

[Glancing away] He's – he can be very hard . . . sometimes. You don't wanna be gettin' him mad. He's strict, but we never object. That's how he wants it, so we go along. He shows us the value of work and hard effort.

So your very first public performance was in a shopping centre?

Well, I sang at my school, a long, long time ago. At a P.T.A. meeting I sung Climb Every Mountain. And boy, did I hear some applause. Those claps, I can still hear them now – really. All the teachers were there. I felt proud. I was five. I think my music teacher taught me the words.

I had a music class, but I never paid attention in that class. [Laughs] I went to the Garnet Grammar School on Garnet Street. We lived on Jackson Street. Pure coincidence.

What was it like being so young and travelling around performing in those early days?

We had our own van. It was some great times. I would sit in the wings and watch the other acts, on and on. I would watch every step Jackie Wilson made on the stage. I'd hear them say, "Jackie Wilson!" And he would take that coat off and strut around! I would sit there and watch every step and just *learn*. Every show, I would run down just to watch him take the stage.

We had our own band, and we would tour with the O'Jays when there used to be four O'Jays, and the Emotions – we been knowing them girls for *years*. We always knew they were great, and now they're just happening. People say, "Oh them. A new group." I'd say, "That's what you think. They been around a *long* time."

Were these tours package deals a record company put together?

I don't think they were on our company [*Motown*]. They just did the shows. We'd tour the East: We did the Regal Theater in Chicago, the Apollo in New York, the Uptown in Philadelphia. That's mainly the ones I remember.

Where do you play now when you tour?

We just finished a big concert tour; we were in England. We did a command performance for the Queen in Scotland, and we went to Germany, to Paris, to Holland. I wish we could have filmed it, because we keep a catalogue of shows. I'll never forget my first Hollywood Palace Show – or the first time we were on The Ed Sullivan Show. I got it on tape. I'll show you.

[He gets up from his chair and goes to his large, shelved tape library.]

Is that a Star Wars cassette you've got there?

Yeah! Barry White, who's on 20th Century Fox Records, got it for us. It's so hard to get into that movie.

But anyway [*cuing up 1970 Ed Sullivan tape*], Motown would tape all their TV shows, but CBS dubbed this one up for me.

I'll never forget the day I was walking the halls at the Ed Sullivan Theater. I walked past his dressing room – see, I'm always known for just looking around and seeing what each place is like; I always do that. And he calls me in, and he says he saw our rehearsal that day, and said, "No matter what you do, never forget to thank God for your talent." He looked me in the eyes. He was unique, he was really kind. Such a nice man.

[Tape begins. Ed Sullivan, a bundle of nervous ticks and furtive movements, stands at stage right and announces, "From Gary, Indiana, here's the youthful Jackson 5, opening with a medley of their hits that have sold over a million, each, er, skit-bit!" The group begins performing I Want You Back.

Michael stands and stares at his younger, diminutive self on the screen, dressed in a garish citrus-coloured vest and bell-bottoms, executing a series of intricate dance steps as he sings. Watching himself, the modern-day Michael appears riveted.]

Do you remember this song?

Are you kidding? Of course I do.

How old are you there?

Eleven.

The music was prerecorded, wasn't it?

[Still watching as a group goes into ABC] I was singing live. The background is pre-recorded. I always had to do that. I was always worried about these shows, because if you mess up, everybody see it. You had to be really on your toes.

[The onscreen Michael goes into a superbly dextrous dance break, dipping, whirling, and shouting, "Sit down, girl! I think I love you. No! Get up, girl! Show me what you can do!" The other Jackson brothers lip-sync the backing chorus: "Shake it, shake it, baby." Then Michael sings the final refrain: "A-B-C, it's easy, it's like counting up to three. Sing a simple melody. That's how easy love can be!" The music stops, and Michael shouts, "A-B-C, girls!"

Off-camera, throngs of little girls in the studio audience shriek.

ED SULLIVAN: On July 7, these five brothers will begin their summer tour of one-nighters at Madison Square Garden, and they're gonna bust every record in the country. Wonderful to have you on our show!

MICHAEL AND BROTHERS: Thank you.

ED SULLIVAN: Right now, here they are singing The Love You Save from their new album, ABC!

Little Michael's onscreen steps are spectacular during the opening instrumental passage of the track, the routine a tightly plotted explosion of springs, spins, shimmies, and jitterbugging fandangos. The real Michael looks bored, and shuts off the tape.]

When was the last time you watched this video clip?

[Long, nervous pause] I've watched it . . . before.

I recall seeing the Jackson 5 on TV in 1974, at the time of Dancing Machine. You had a dance routine that was so wickedly hot. Do you put those things together yourself?

Do you mean the robot moves and all that? We always do all our own choreography. Michael, Marlon, and Jackie, us three do it.

You always had great moves. I'm sure you had a lot of people coming up to you and saying you were very skilled for your age. I don't know of any eleven-year-old kids who had that kind of poise.

[Glum, exasperated] For so many years I've been called a midget, a 45-year-old midget, and I was, like, six and five. And they would tell us how "great, great, great" we were, but could "never get the big head". We heard that so much. *"Never get the big head."* They were saying don't get too big for your shoes.

Have you ever gotten a big head?

Oh, no. No way. No way I could deal with that.

Why do you think that is? Because your father tells you to be cool? Or your brothers do?

Yeah. Good parents, and just, you know, how can you think you're better than somebody else? I mean, I do certain things that millions of kids out there will never get to see or do, but I shouldn't think I'm better than them. *[In a hush]* We're all human.

Have you ever had kids your own age approach you and remark on your amazing abilities? How would you react?

I'd just listen – and then get better and better.

I don't know what I was thinking back then. I'd just listen, say thanks, and keep on going, and not let it affect me terribly anyway. *[Suddenly tense]* I'm just always trying to get better. That's all, really. I'm just telling you that all I'm trying to do is get better and better. Which I never stop doing. 'Cause when you stop growing . . . [He cancels the thought]. Boy, you never can stop growing. But some people do.

On TV you look sharply accomplished, even shrewd. And tough, almost like a grown man. But I meet you now, and there's a striking difference.

[Smiling strangely] That's true. People always tell me that. All the kids at school say, "Man, you're so much different on stage. I can't believe it's the same person." But I'm not really recognizing what people are telling me.

When I get on stage, I don't know what happens. Honest to God. It feels so good, it's like it's the safest place in the world for me. [Warily] I'm not as comfortable now as I would be on stage, because I was raised on stage. That's all I did: travel, sing, dance and watch other people that were trying to do it.

At school, I didn't know how to be in class. Teachers would write home and say [giggles], "Michael comes to school to sleep." Because we would be up all night in the nightclubs, doing our acts and tours. When I'd get to school, that'd be my sleeping hours.

[Confidential tone] And my pockets would be *loaded* with money. Because people would throw money on the stage – the money, the change! We would have $1,300 lying on the stage, and we would make just $15 from the manager paying us. We'd go to school – *whoa!* – with all this money.

It was great, great times. [Dreamily] I'll never forget those times. I write about them in songs.

I'm writing a lot now, too.

These days you're writing a lot of songs?

[Nodding] In the studio. I love to go into sessions and listen. Whenever Stevie [Wonder] has a session, I'm always there. I sit and listen and *learn*. He's a great friend of mine, and I think he's one of the greatest guys around. He's so much farther ahead of everybody; he's so good.

What kinds of topics are you writing about these days?

[Cool, pensive] I just *hate* everyday love songs. I'm interested in a different type of love song. I want a brand-new thought.

That's what I love about Ben. There's a mystery to it. You wonder, "What is this about?" I even got sick of it *[snigger]*, so many people come up to me and say, "Why did you create such a song about a little stinkin' rat? But it's so beautiful! How'd you make it so beautiful if it's about a dumb rat?"

I said, "I don't know. I just felt it, because rats, they got a mind, they got a heart as well." I don't look at it that way. I *love* animals, I said, "*You* may not look at it that way, but I love animals."

I write about all kinda things. I write about an old man, a tree, what's happening in the world, a deer. I love writing so much I'd *eat* it, really. I love it!

Have you ever written a song about one very specific incident? You met someone, something very specific occurred, you wrote about it – and maybe it went on to be a hit?

Oh yeah. A song I'm writing now about travelling the world. It mentions, in the song, all the different countries, and to me, what they're like. And there are so many people around the world that *don't* get a chance to travel. And there are some that *do* want to travel but can't. And some that think the whole world looks like New York City, that the whole world is what they just picture. There are a lot of people like that.

Well, some do say that Europe is looking too much like America, from McDonald's hamburger stands on outward.

Oh, not to me. Did you go out in the country and stuff? Now, business *will* do that, but that different country and their society and their culture just creeps in anyway. The governments are different, and there's no way that could be like America. Of course, business will remind you – you look at McDonald's sometime and you forget that you're in England. But they even have McDonald's stands that look different! So there's no way: The culture is different, the government is different, the countryside is different.

Nonetheless, other countries put such a value on the American system – the way we think, the way we dress – because they consider us the most current in a lot of ways.

Americans got it made. They got it *made*. I don't think the different governments would let that happen. I know they have their ways of doing things, and they're completely different from what Americans do.

Have you ever been to Holland? Holland is the Europe that you *dream* about – I'm not just saying this. London, England's city, *can* look like New York – a little – but if you go to Holland, man, you know it's real Europe. And Scotland is – oh, I could eat it, it's so beautiful! You know it's not America.

Back to your records: Is there a big hit that came out of a personal experience I might not necessarily pick out from the song itself?

If so, I would write it out on the album jacket, and talk about it. See, we just started writing songs on our albums. Before, those songs were all by Motown producers. We would help in, but we would never mainly write the stories or anything. With our singing, we would help in. That's what so great about what we're doing now. We *will* be writing our own stuff, completely.

How about Goin' Places?

That was a tune Kenny Gamble [and Leon Huff] wrote. We wrote Different Kind Of Lady and Do What You Wanna. But they wasn't specific to something that happened in our lives.

See, I love the folk type of style music, the soul, and the rhythm going out funky. I like to mix those things. And I like easy listening. I like Bread, the Carpenters. I love Stevie Wonder and the Brothers Johnson – they are smelly, they are really *smelly*. Strawberry Letter 23, that track is bad, isn't it? The lyrics are – **cripes**, they're so way out, they're crazy! I'm still trying to figure them out.

Have you ever seen Parliament-Funkadelic with their flying saucer-Dr. Funkenstein show? They're pretty off-the-wall.

I'm 'posta see them in concert. I *know* they crazy. But I'm gonna watch carefully to see if it's them that's good live, or just the scenery and special effects.

Was there one person who was a model or hero of yours when you were forging your own particular style?

I had those that I admired, like James Brown, a man that today don't get the credit he should get from the music industry. Look what he did to music: all these funky tracks that you hear today, that's where it came from. Sly Stone, James Brown, these are people that started funky music. They stood between the gospelly soul and the dance music. And that's *funk*: Sly, James Brown, and people like that. Wilson Pickett, Otis Redding. And of course in rock and roll there's Little Richard and Chuck Berry and all those guys. That's who I would always watch. And Jackie Wilson – *yeow*!

Have you met James Brown?

I know James Brown. I met him long time ago at the Regal Theater. I don't remember exactly how – *[fretting]* how could I forget? I just remember him on stage gettin' down.

I talked with him during rehearsal at a Dick Clark music awards show last year. He said, "I remember you back at the Apollo Theater. I'm the one who got you the gig! One of your biggest breaks!" I said, "Thank you." He read me the cash receipts from his last tour, and then he broke out into the aisle, sliding and doing the James Brown dance. And then he walked off. *[Laughs]*

But you know, rock and roll, at one time, nobody even wanted to hear it. *[Laughs]* They said, "What *is* this?"

Elvis was considered white trash for singing so-called race music in his hillbilly style.

See, but when the blacks did it, they really wouldn't accept it. It's only a fact, and it's true. It turned around when people like Elvis did it, but it was there all the time. Blacks had been doing it for years.

Mostly everybody made fun of it. There's this book called Blues: The Devil's Music, and it talks about the origination of blues, and how people just talked so *bad* about it. And look what it is today! Even with the rock and roll, as well. And jazz.

When did you go over to visit with Jackie Wilson?

When we did our album; we just finished it. Not too long ago, in Philadelphia, at the hospital. He really don't get the credit he should get. He's the man the big people of today in the music industry copy after. *[After years of hospitalization following an on stage heart attack in 1975, Wilson died in 1984.]*

Does that bother you?

Yes. I think it's an *awful* thing. 'Cause I like the people who really do something; they sweat and work for it and go through hell bringing it about. And the guy who takes it so quick *[loudly snaps his fingers]*, he comes along and gets all the credit for it. I'm glad at least it took somebody to bring it about, but real people should get credit.

Same thing with artists that paint. It happens the same way – till they die, and then they get the recognition.

Have you ever felt that way about things you've done?

Yeah, a lot of things. *[Giggles]* You know, I don't have to mention names. How do I feel about it? I feel it's a compliment in one way, and in another way *[voice drops to a whisper]* you be kinda *angry*.

[Aggressive] Because it's *yours*. We were the first young group out there with that style, making hit records. There were nobody out there at our age. We came across it, and then all of a sudden along came the Osmonds, the Partridge Family.

Now you have groups like the Sylvers! The Sylvers have the same producer that wrote all our hits, Freddie Perren. That's why they sound so much like us.

A lot of people that worked with the Osmonds said they would have videotapes on us and study us. They really patterned themselves after us, because they were singing barbershop on The Andy Williams Show. They never were recording jams, poppin' soul, then – boom! – they were.

I heard One Bad Apple several times before I found out it wasn't you people.

[Grinning fiercely] I know! One lady walked up to me and said, "I got your new record." I said, "What?" She said, "One Bad Apple." I said, "Lady, why don't you *read* who's on the label?"

Did you know that record was ours at first? But Motown turned it down. George Jackson is the producer, and he came to Motown with it, and Motown turned it down. Because we were in a funky, strong track-type bag, with good melody. George's song was good, but too easygoing; we were striving for something much stronger. So he went and gave it to the Osmonds. *[Annoyed]* They sang it, and it was a smash – Number 1.

He had you in mind when he wrote it?

Sure! That's why it was mainly like us all the way. They sounded so much like us. I don't mind if somebody takes it and go farther with it. The only thing I *hate* is they take it and make like they started it. It's like a dog-eat-dog type of situation. I think it's *aw-ful*.

At least The Beatles did mention where they were influenced. They were great writers, on their own, but they *did* study black music. 'Cause Chuck Berry – who was it, Chuck Berry or Little Richard? – when The Beatles were coming up he saw them and he introduced them to a lot of people. A long time ago, The Beatles were on an all-black label *[Vee-Jay]*. The guy's name is [Ewart] Abner – I know him, he was president of Motown Records – and a long time ago, he had them! Then, after they went on from there, they were gigantic.

I love Paul McCartney. With his own records he proves he's the most talented Beatle. When you take any one of them away, it gets kinda weaker and weaker, but as a whole, it was always the best. Paul – him and John Lennon were dynamite. I've been to two of Paul's parties, and we get together and talk.

He wrote a song for me, and I never get a chance to record it. Him and his wife were telling me about it. It's called Girlfriend. *[Girlfriend was included by McCartney on Wings' 1978 London Town album. Michael finally recorded the song in 1979 for his Off The Wall LP.]* They were singing it to me, and they say they want to do it, too.

[He sings] "Girlfriend . . . boyfriend" – it was an easy thing. I remember him singing it. I'll never forget the melody. I can forget all kinds of things *[giggles]*, but I never forget a melody.

This was a year ago. I've got some pictures here of the party. It was a *gigantic* party at the Harold Lloyd estate. It was a very good evening. All the stars were there! *[He pulls a voluminous black scrapbook off a nearby shelf and leafs through it.]* Lemme see. This is when we met the Queen . . . This is at Paul's party at

Harold Lloyd's estate, right around the time when Paul and his wife and I, were were talking about the Girlfriend song, and exchanging numbers and addresses.

That was one of the greatest parties I've ever been to, because when Paul gives a party he believes in just *going out*! It was a whole schedule: nine o'clock, you get to see the ballerina act. Ten o'clock, Chuck Norris, the karate expert, put on a show. At four o'clock in the evening, the Broadway company of The Wiz would put on a show. There were all kinds of food! You want Mexican food, they had a Mexican stand, a Mexican lady. Italian, and Italian stand with an Italian man. American food, a buffet! Oh, man!

And that's more at Paul McCartney's party, where they had the Wiz show... And John Belushi doing his Joe Cocker imitation at Paul's thing, too. Did you see the robot on summer TV specials? That was the same robot that was at Paul McCartney's party! That was the first time I had seen it. I said, "How does he work?" People went crazy over him. And that's my friend Tatum O'Neal . . . And that's my nephew on my brother's side.

I left kinda early, but the party went on and on . . .

Do you keep a lot of scrapbooks like this?

[Flashing a confused glance, continuing to thumb through it] Not really. We have somebody in the business office who makes them up for me, and our own photographer to follow me and take the pictures . . . That's my father's father, Samuel Jackson, and that's the three brothers that had the band the Falcons: Lawrence, Joseph, and Luke . . . Samuel Jackson still around the house; he sings and sings; he's still alive in Arizona. And that's the first monkey on the moon! She's still alive today. Her name is Miss Baker. *[He points to an odd scrawl below the shot of the chimp.]* See, she "autographed" it. It's good to look back and think. There's Fred Astaire . . . and Minnie Riperton . . . *[He puts the scrapbook away.]*

Tomorrow, from when you wake up, what will your schedule for the day be like?

I get up at 9.00am or 8.30, and I work on The Wiz at the

rehearsals until 5.30pm. Then I'm free, unless I have other appointments. I'm going to the Parliament-Funkadelic concert tomorrow, which is a form of freedom, but there's no way I can get away from the stage completely. I got to have it!

Certain people were created for certain things, and I think our job is to entertain the world. I don't see no other thing that I could be doing.

So many people do so many different things that they're good at. It seems like "He was meant to do that!" or "That's her job!" because of how they enjoy it. It's that way with me and entertainment, and it's strange, because our whole family is in on this thing. We all do it.

I notice the Bible over on the coffee table. Is your family especially religious?

We all believe in God, of course. *[Giggles]* I study and read the Bible with my mother and sisters. I know there's a true and breathing God. A lot of people don't believe in that, but I know there's *no way* it can't be. There's no way it couldn't be; it's so true that there is a God, when you break it down: the universe, the beauty of the world, the sun.

But there's a lot of ugliness in the world, too, a lot of cruelty. Did God create that?

No! That's because of man! Man is because of the fallen angels. It says in the Bible that all this would happen, and it's all coming true.

It's easy to judge the world from the privileged safety of America. If you'd been to India, say, and seen the ugliness there…

I can't wait! That's what I *want* to see! I've seen the very rich and the very poor, but I'm mainly interested in the poor. I don't wanna think the whole world is just like what's around here. I want to appreciate what I have, and try to help others.

I know what the rich are like. I've studied that country India so much, and when I go to other countries, people say, "You wanna see the ugly part of it?" *[Nods]* That's what I want to see!

What are you looking for?

[Smiling] I want to see what it's really like to *starve*. I don't want to hear it, or read it. I want to see it.

Why?

It's a whole different thing when you see it! All the things I've read in my schoolbooks about England and the Queen were OK, but my very eyes are the greatest book in the world. When we did the Royal Command Performance over in England, and then after it I actually looked into the Queen's eyes, it was the greatest thing! And it's really the same thing with starvation! *[Dreamily]* When you see it, you just receive a little more.

What would you say is the worst thing you ever saw in your life?

Well, can it be anything?

Sure.

It was probably during the hard days on stage. Some of the things I use ta see when we used to do nightclub acts. *[Giggles]* You'll probably say, "Aw, that ain't nothing," but to me, especially at that age, I had never seen anything like it.

Seen what?

[Giggling harder] See, we used to do club shows, and there was this one lady – you probably know what she did – but I thought it was awful. I was around six, and she was one of those stripteasers, and she would take her drawers off *[giggles]*, and a man would come up, and they'd start doing – aw, man, she was too funky! Ugh! That, to me, was *awful*!

Looking backward and forward, how do you feel about your body of work?

All those records in the past are our songs, and we've sung them, and we put our hearts into the *singing* of them, but they're really not from *us*. They're not *our* thoughts and what we think should go on that plastic, on that wax.

When I get into writing my own stuff, I'm gonna just let it *all* out. It's something I always wanted to do: Make it really *me*!

Speaking of your thoughts and your heart, do you have any girlfriends?

I'm too busy for dating and girls right now. I'd like to try, maybe. What do *you* think? Think I should, yeah? Well, I'll think about that. I'll think about what you said. We'll see . . . But I'm happy.

You've certainly got the power to make yourself happy. People live their whole lives and don't find that power. Do you think you'll use it well?

[*Grim-faced, listing his thoughts on his fingers*] OK. For starters, there's nothing inside of me that wants to come out but don't know how. I just let it all come out.

If there's something I'm not, I'll mention it.

I love children – crazy 'bout 'em.

I love music.

I'm looking forward to writing lots of songs and good material and putting it out and just doing my best.

So nothing's bothering me, because I got things that I want to do, and I know I can do them.

[*Adamant*] There's nothing inside killing me.

Filming The Wiz and playing the Scarecrow seem to be the high points of your life thus far. Will you be sad to see it end?

[*Musing, almost whispering*] Ohhh yeah. Sometimes, when I come home with my make-up, I keep dancing in front of the mirrors here as the Scarecrow. Or I get out of bed at night and do a few moves in front of the mirrors.

When I get into it, I forget everything else but the Scarecrow's world. It's a feeling of peace. It's just like . . . magic.

IN THEIR OWN WORDS

Among the most successful of Omnibus Press's innovations has been the In Their Own Words series. The utter simplicity of the idea – the wit and hopefully wisdom of an artist or band collected, divided up under thematic headings and presented with almost no comment by the collator/editor – has meant that the books function equally comfortably as pure entertainment or works of reference. The number of artists who've received the Own Words treatment now approaches two dozen. We've chipped away suitably juicy chunks of the best of them. There's Freddie Mercury holding forth on his favourite topic, Freddie Mercury (the book originally edited by Mick St Michael), Led Zeppelin on their classic fourth album (Paul Kendall), Bruce Springsteen's reflections on Born To Run (John Duffy), Bob Dylan dissecting the nature of fame (Chris Williams), high-spirited press conference antics with The Beatles (Miles), Guns N'Roses on the booze (Mark Putterford), Keith Richards on the joy of hard drugs (David Dalton and Mick Farren) and The Doors on the night Jim Morrison exposed himself in Miami (Andrew Doe and John Tobler) . . .

THE DOORS ON 'THAT' INCIDENT

Jim: There are no rules at a rock concert. Anything is possible. *(1969)*

Larry Mahoney (Miami Herald): It was the night of the riot that did not happen. The Doors, a theatrical rock group, and singer Jim Morrison, pulled out all the stops in an abortive effort to provoke chaos among a huge crowd of Miami young people packed into the Dinner Key Auditorium at $6 a head. The hypnotically erotic Morrison, flouting the laws of obscenity, indecent exposure and incitement to riot, could only stir a minor mob scene towards the end of his Saturday night performance.

Many of the nearly 12,000 youths said they found the bearded singer's exhibition disgusting. Included in the audience were hundreds of unescorted junior and senior high girls. The Dinner Key exhibition lasted one hour and five minutes. For this, The Doors were paid $25,000. Morrison sang only one song, and that was off-key. For the remainder, he grunted and groaned, gyrated and gestured, in a manner that made Elvis Presley's style seem more staid than a Presbyterian preacher's. His words were inflammatory in a tightly packed crowd . . . It was not meant to be pretty.

Morrison appeared to masturbate in full view of his audience, screamed obscenities and exposed himself. He also got violent, slugged several officials and threw one of them off the stage before he himself was hurled into the crowd. Morrison, as he does in most of his shows, stole the hat of one of the policemen. The officer wandered about on the stage during the climax of the show trying to get it back. At no time was any effort made by the police to arrest Morrison, even when the mob scene on the bandstand got out of hand. Nor was a report made to headquarters on what had happened. Morrison, who left Miami on Sunday, may yet be arrested for the exhibition, Acting Police Chief Paul M. Denham said. *(1969)*

Jim: At Miami, I tried to reduce the myth to absurdity, thereby wiping it out. It just got too much for me to stomach, so I put an end to it one glorious night. I told the audience that they were a bunch of idiots to be members of a crowd, and what were they doing there anyway? Not to listen to some songs by a bunch of good musicians, but for something else . . . so why not admit it and do something about it? *(1969)*

Robbie: All I remember was, it was a real hot night in Miami. We played at this place called the Dinner Key Auditorium, which was used, I think, more for political meetings and stuff, rather than rock concerts. There was no air conditioning or anything, so by the time we went on stage, the place was a madhouse already – the kids were drunk, or on angel dust, something like that. The place was crazed. Before we went on stage, we were upstairs in the dressing room, and there were a number of policemen up there, and we were joking with them and everything, having a good time.

So, we finally went down and started to play, and Jim was in one of his more evil moods that night, I would have to say. He'd just had a fight with his girlfriend that day, which didn't exactly help matters . . . and what happened was, there was a lot of confusion on stage. We didn't play one of our best sets, I have to admit. I remember starting one of the songs about three times before we finally got into it – but the kids were having a great time. They were laughing and boogying around. And the allegation is that Jim whipped it out, in front of the audience, right? Well, I personally never saw that happen, nor did Ray or John, and out of the two or three hundred photographs that were taken that night, there's not one shot that shows that happening.

There was a lot of movement on stage, jumping around, and finally Jim jumped into the audience. People were just milling around – it looked like a scene from that movie, The Snake Pit, where people were rushing around in endless waves. I don't know what Ray did, but finally John and I scooted off stage at that point, because someone was yelling that it was about to collapse, so we beat it upstairs. I don't know how Jim got out of there, but he finally managed to get back out of the audience, and upstairs. He was pretty high by that point, I must confess, and he grabbed one of the cop's hats and was fooling around with it . . . and the cops were in a good mood, so we finally left.

We all went off to Jamaica for a while, for a little rest, and when we got back, we found a warrant out for Jim's arrest. We didn't know what it was for, and nobody else did either. Finally we learned what had allegedly happened – and that was what the whole Miami trial was about. *(1978)*

Ray: Jim said to the audience, 'That's enough. You didn't come here to hear music, you didn't come to see a good rock'n'roll band – you came here for something you've never seen before, something greater and bigger than you've ever experienced. What can I do? How 'bout if I show you my cock? Isn't that what you want?' So he took his shirt off and put it in front of himself, and started dancing around holding his shirt down, covering his groin . . . and then he pulled his shirt away and said, 'Did ya see it, did ya see it? There it is! Look! I did it, I did it!' *(1981)*

Ray: I don't think he ever really did it . . . no-one knows for sure. I was five to eight feet away from Jim on stage, and I always have a tendency to put my head down. I'm not concerned with what Jim is doing physically on stage. We didn't have to look at each other – we weren't communicating on that plane . . . so same thing in Miami. I wasn't really looking. He said to me the next day, 'Did I do anything wrong?' And he played along; whether he was putting us on or not, we'll never know, because he looked us right in the eyes and said, 'I don't remember a thing. I had a lot of drinks and I don't even remember getting to Miami.' So who knows? He may have been absolutely honest in that he didn't remember anything. *(1980)*

Jim *(attributed)*: Uh-oh, I think I exposed myself out there. *(1969)*

John: We didn't get any support from the rock'n'roll community. They seemed glad. *(1972)*

'The Lords': But most of the press were vultures, descending on the scene for curious America.

Ray: It was a chance for the righteous to punish those whom they considered unrighteous. There was so much indignation, there was no sense in talking to them. 'You are on the side of the wrong,' they stated, and that was that! It was also a chance for them to make plenty of political hay. *(1980)*

Jim: This trial, and its outcome, won't change my style, because I maintain that I didn't do anything wrong . . . It's actually a very fascinating thing to go through, a thing you can observe. If I have to go to jail, I hope the others will go on and create an instrumental sound of their own, one that doesn't depend on lyrics. Lyrics aren't really that essential in music, anyway. *(1969)*

Jim: I don't know what will happen. I'd guess we'll carry on like this for a while then, to get our vitality back, maybe we'll have to get out of the whole business . . . maybe go to an island by ourselves and start creating again. I might put some of it in a song . . . but the trouble is, the outcome wasn't clear-cut enough for that. *(1969)*

Jim: I was just fed up with the image that had been created around me, which I co-operated with, sometimes consciously, mostly unconsciously. *(1969)*

Jim: Let's just say I was testing the bounds of reality. I was curious to see what would happen. That's all it was: curiosity. *(1969)*

GUNS N'ROSES: DRINK N'DRUGS

Slash: I have a tendency to get really drunk and then I get to the hotel and I'll pick the first chick up that I can get. You'd be surprised at some of the chicks I've picked up. *(1988)*

Duff: There's a time to do drugs and there's a time to drink and there's a time to do what you've got to do . . . And you've got to realise the difference. *(1991)*

Slash: I just liked it (heroin). I liked the way it felt. And fuck, I didn't know if I did it four or five days in a row I'd get fucking hooked on it! And that's a different subject altogether. That drug takes you over mentally and physically, so much that to come back is hard. I was never a big coke addict, ever. *(1991)*

Slash: You know, there are some people in this business who take drugs just cause they'd get fat if they drank. They should join us and go on The Jack Daniel's Plan! *(1992)*

Slash: It (drinking) is a habit I picked up when I was 12 years old. It helps me, it brings me out of my shell, because I cannot deal with people in a social situation when I'm sober. If I don't have a drink, I sink into myself. And I like it! I like being drunk, it's fun. I'm usually quite a good drinker, though I admit I can be a bit obnoxious when I'm drunk sometimes. *(1988)*

Slash: I get hassled for, like, drinking Black Death. Influencing the youth of America. What?! I didn't know that was my gig! *(1992)*

Slash: The afternoon we found out we would have to quit the (Iron) Maiden tour, I went around grabbing every bottle of Jack I could find stashed around our dressing room and took it all back to the hotel. That was five days ago and I've been living off it ever since. But now I'm down to my last bottle and a half. After that, I guess I'll be back to buying my own . . . *(1988)*

Slash: When we get up in the afternoon to do a soundcheck, we drink so much that we can't play, because our hands are shaking like windmills. So what happens? We drink! We drink more and more, and then we're fine, and we wake up the next day with some floosie . . . you don't know her name . . . you've got weird shit on your dick . . . your bed's all wet from pissing in it, and you go, "Listen, will you do me a favour and find me some booze and some pizza?" *(1987)*

Axl: Drinking hurts my throat. *(1988)*

Slash: A bottle (of Jack Daniel's) a day for five years, that's what I was doing . . . you have really bad breath in the morning . . . you know, you can't have sex in the morning till you've brushed your teeth, which is a real fucking drag. *(1988)*

Slash: I drink a bottle of Jack Daniel's a day. Am I gonna die? *(1988)*

Slash: If you were to ask, as a therapist, 'Why do I drink?' . . . the simple thing is you do it out of boredom and to relax. The worst thing is it's for people who are so volatile and so shy . . . you end up drinking a lot to come out of your shell. In that way it's a vicious sort of drug, because it works. *(1991)*

Slash: You just gotta keep the shit in check. I've been drinking a lot for a long time and I'm only 23 years old, and I know that, right? It's not something that I'm just so ignorant about that I'm going on this major blow out, until all of a sudden something stops me physically. I'm more aware than that, but I'll do it anyway. So if anything does happen, I won't be complaining about it, 'cos I knew, you know? *(1988)*

Izzy: (Drugs) were doing me in. I felt like shit all the time. I went to somewhere where I knew I couldn't score, I had some Codeine with me and a few Valium to take the edge off, and I basically sweated it out. I made through the 72-hour period but then I started drinking like a fish. I gave that up as well a couple of months later. I've been told that alcohol's no good for American-Indian blood which I've got in me. Alcohol really does fuck me up. It makes me crazy. I become impossible to deal with. I knew that I couldn't afford to fuck up any more. I'd used up all my Get Out Of Jail Free cards. *(1992)*

KEITH RICHARDS ON HARD DRUGS

In guys particularly, junk takes the place of everything. You don't need a chick, you don't need music, you don't need nothing. It doesn't get you anywhere. It's not called junk for nothing. Why did Burroughs kick it, after 25 years?

People have offered me a lot of things over the years, mainly to keep going. "Work, you bastard. Take one of these." I've tried a lot of shit. I don't even know what it is. I personally think . . . it depends if you're ready. Same with alcohol. You should find out what it does. If you don't know what it does and you're just putting it in for the sake of it, you're a dummy.

What it does depends on what form you take it in. Some people snort, some people shoot it. You tell me what it does. The Peruvians, they chew it, and that's the trip. You can buy it in any grocery store and you eat it with a hunk of limestone and it just freezes you. At 11,000 feet it's hard to breathe anyway. Those cats have 47 per cent more red corpuscles than us lowlanders. Huge lungs, and they're chewing it all the time. You buy it along with your eggs and your lemons. It depends how you take it. *(1973)*

I once took that apomorphine cure that Burroughs swears by. Dr. Dent was dead, but his assistant whom he trained, this lovely old dear called Smitty, who's like mother hen, still runs the clinic. I had her down to my place for five days, and she just sort of comes in and says, "Here's your shot, dear, there's a good boy," or "You've been a naughty boy, you've taken something, yes you have, I can tell." But it's a pretty medieval cure. You just vomit all the time.

Electro-acupuncture . . . it's so simple it's not true. But as to whether or not they'll ever let people know about it is another thing. I can't tell you how it works because they don't even know for sure. All they know is that it does work. It's a little metal box with leads that clip on to your ears, and in two or three days . . . which is the worst period for licking junk . . . in those 72 hours it leaves your system.

Actually, you should be incredibly sick, but for some reason you're not. Why? I don't know, because all it is is a very simple electronic nine volt battery-run operation. *(1978)*

Do you regret starting to take hard drugs?
No, I don't regret nuthin'. I just got bored with it. It would take more than the Mounties to turn me off something. If I really wanted to stay on it, I'd stay on it. Because I know damn well that in prison you can get as much as you want. When I was in prison in England in 1967, my first day there, another inmate tapped me on the shoulder and asked me if I wanted some hash. That was years ago. Can you imagine what it must be like now? All you've gotta do is bend over twice or have the right amount of tobacco and you've got whatever you want.

But do you feel better mentally now you've given up heroin?
Different and I suppose you could say healthier. Although I must say in fairness to the poppy that never once did I have a cold. The cure for the common cold is there, but they daren't tell anybody because they would have a nation full of dope addicts. I don't recommend drugs to anybody. It's really

wrong when 12-year-olds are on the streets scoring dope with strychnine thrown in to give it an extra flash. The worst thing is the ignorance of people taking things without knowing what they're doing.

You need the freedom and lifestyle to be able to indulge in drugs.
I don't know if it's that. Half the reason I got drawn into it was because I didn't have a lot of freedom and time off. If I'd had the freedom I could have dragged myself off to somewhere remote for three months and cleaned myself up and pulled myself together. But in this business there is always a new tour to do, and before you know it, five years have gone. I started getting hooked 10 years ago. That was when I was into squeezing blackheads! Now I'm pulling out grey hairs – ha ha!

But now I can remember what each show was like afterwards, without having somebody tell me. I did a lot of shows when I was completely out of my brain. One show was just like another, and it was like a tunnel that got smaller and smaller.

I was on and off junk for 10 years. But – and I want to make this clear – that doesn't prescribe it for anybody else. *(1978)*

Originally, that was just an overall observation. I went through it and didn't feel anything in particular . . . I don't know, though. I was 33 last year and the effect has taken a few months to make itself felt. There was that whole Toronto incident and at the end of that I just knew I had to finish with dope. So I guess I did undergo something of a traumatic experience at 33 . . . *(1978)*

You could be sick as a dog but as long as you've got a suntan, everybody thinks you're in great shape. *(1977)*

THE BEATLES' PRESS CONFERENCES

Beethoven figures in one of your songs. What do you think of Beethoven?
Ringo: He's great. Especially his poetry.

Do you believe in lunacy?
Ringo: Yeah; it's healthy.
But aren't you embarrassed by all the lunacy?
Ringo: No, it's crazy.

Ringo, why do you wear two rings on each hand?
Ringo: Because I can't fit them through my nose.

What do you think of Christine Keeler?
Ringo: She's a great comic.

Do you think it's wrong to set such a bad example to teenagers, smoking the way you do?
Ringo: It's better than being alcoholics.

What do you think of the criticism that you are not very good?
George: We're not.

What do you believe is the reason you are the most popular singing group today?
John: We've no idea. If we did, we'd get four long-haired boys, put them together and become their managers.

You've admitted to being agnostics. Are you also irreverent?
Paul: We are agnostics so there is no point in being irreverent.

What did you think when your airliner's engine began smoking as you landed today?
Ringo: Beatles, women and children first!

What kind of things annoy you?
Paul: Nothing annoys us really. Some things make us laugh. Like those "Stamp out The Beatles!" gags. And the other day a photographer asked if he could take two pictures of us – one with our wigs on and one with our wigs off.

Why do teenagers stand up and scream piercingly and painfully when you appear?
Paul: None us of know. But we've heard that teenagers go to our shows just to scream. A lot of them don't even want to listen because they have our records. We kind of like the screaming teenagers. If they want to pay their money and sit out there and shout, that's their business. We aren't going to be like little dictators and say, "You've got to shut up." The commotion doesn't bother us any more. It's come to be like working in a bell factory. You don't hear the bells after a while.

What is your personal goal?
George: To do as well as I can at whatever I attempt. And someday to die with a peaceful mind.
But you really don't expect that to happen for a long time yet, do you?
George: When your number's up, it's up.

Do you plan to marry Jane Asher?
Paul: I've got no plans. But everybody keeps saying I have. Maybe they know better. They say I'm married and divorced and have 50 kids . . .

What kind of music do you like?
Paul: Coloured American groups.

What started your practice of wearing four rings at once?
Ringo: Six got to be too heavy.

Why do you think you get more fan mail than anyone else in the group?

Ringo: I dunno. I suppose it's because more people write to me.

Do you date much?
Ringo: What are you doing tonight?

Do you fight amongst yourselves?
John: Only in the mornings.

What do you miss most now that your fame prohibits your freedom?
Ringo: Going to the movies.
George: Having nothing to do.
John: School, because you don't have much to do there.
Paul: Going on buses.

What impresses you most about America?
John: Bread.
Paul: Going on buses.

On arriving in the USA ...

How do you like this welcome?
Ringo: So this is America. They all seem out of their minds.

What do you do when you're cooped up in a hotel room between shows?
George: We ice skate.

Why are your speaking voices different from your singing voices?
George: We don't have a musical background.

Do you like fish and chips?
Ringo: Yes, but I like steak and chips better.

How tall are you?
Ringo: Two feet, nine inches.

Paul, what do you think of columnist Walter Winchell?
Paul: He said I'm married and I'm not.
George: Maybe he wants to marry you . . .

How did you find America?
Ringo: We went to Greenland and made a left turn.

Would you like to walk down the street without being recognised?
John: We used to do this with no money in our pockets.
There's no point in it.

Are you scared when crowds scream at you?
John: More so in Dallas than in other places perhaps.

Is it true you can't sing?
John [*points to George*]: Not me. Him.

Why don't you smile, George?
George: I'll hurt my lips.

What's your reaction to a Seattle psychiatrist's opinion that you are a menace?
George: Psychiatrists are a menace.

What's this about an annual illness, George?
George: I get cancer every year.

Where would you like to go if all the security wasn't necessary?
John: Harlem.

How do you feel about other Beatle-type groups?
John: The Rolling Stones are personal friends of ours. They are most creative and beginning to write good songs.

Do you like being Beatles?
John: Yes, or we'd be The Rolling Stones.

Do you plan to record any anti-war songs?
John: All our songs are anti-war.

When you do a new song, how do you decide who sings the lead?
John: We just get together and whoever knows most of the words sings the lead.

How do you keep your psychic balance?
Ringo: The important thing is not to get potty. There's four of us so, whenever one of us gets a little potty the other three bring him back to earth.

What do you think you've contributed to the musical field?
Ringo: Records.
George: A laugh and a smile.

How does it feel putting on the whole world?
Ringo: We enjoy it.
Paul: We aren't really putting you on.
George: Just a bit of it.
John: How does it feel to be put on?

Does all the adulation from teenage girls affect you?
John: When I feel my head start to swell, I look at Ringo and know perfectly well we're not supermen.

What's your reaction to composer Aaron Copland who found The Beatles' music interesting and Richard Rodgers who found it boring?
Paul: I like anyone who says he likes our music. I don't mind Richard Rodgers saying he finds it boring but I must add that I find Richard Rodgers's music boring. And I'm not being nasty, Richard.

How do you feel about a nightclub, Arthur, named after your hairstyle?
George: I was proud – until I saw the nightclub.

What do you consider the most important thing in life?
George: Love.

Do you resent fans ripping up your sheets for souvenirs?
Ringo: No I don't mind. So long as I'm not in them while the ripping is going on.

Paul: I once knew a fellow on the Dingle who had two dads. He used to call them number one dad and number two dad. Now apparently number one dad wasn't nice. He used to throw the boy on the fire – which can develop a lot of complexes in a young lad.
Ringo: I remember my uncle putting the red-hot poker on me, and that's no lie. He was trying to frighten me.
Paul: Tell me, Ringo, do all your relatives go around applying red-hot pokers to you?
John: It's the only way they can identify him.
Paul: You see, Ringo comes from a depressed area.
John: Some people call it the slums.
Ringo: No, the slums are farther.

Paul: At school we had a great hip English master and instead of keeping us to the drag stuff like Return Of The Native he would let us read Tennessee Williams and Lady Chatterley's Lover and The Miller's Tale.

John: I get spasms of being intellectual. I read a bit about politics but I don't think I'd vote for anyone. No message from any of those phoney politicians is coming through to me.

George: We've always had laughs. Sometimes we find ourselves hysterical, especially when we're tired. We laugh at soft remarks that the majority of people don't get.

John: The thing I'm afraid of is growing old. I hate that. You get old and you've missed it somehow. The old always resent the young and vice-versa.

Ringo: I'd like to end up sort of unforgettable.

John: Ours is a today image.

What's the most unusual request you've had?
John: I wouldn't like to say.

Ringo: I don't like talking. It's how I'm built. Some people gab all day and some people play it smogo. I don't mind talking or smiling. It's just, I don't do it very much. I haven't got a smiling face or a talking mouth.

John: We're not going to fizzle out in half a day. But afterwards I'm not going to change into a tap dancing musical. I'll just develop what I'm doing at the moment, although whatever I say now I'll change my mind next week. I mean, we all know that bit about "It won't be the same when you're 25". I couldn't care less. This isn't show business. It's something else. This is different from anything that anybody imagines. You don't go on from this. You do this and then you finish.

At the Royal Command Variety Performance at the Prince of Wales Theatre in Piccadilly Circus with the Queen Mother and Princess Margaret present . . .

John: On this next number I want you all to join in. Would those in the cheap seats clap their hands? The rest of you can rattle your jewellery.

Afterwards, The Beatles were presented to the Queen Mother. She asked them where they would be performing next. At Slough, they told her. "Ah," she said with delight, "that's near us."

BBC: How important is it to succeed here [in Paris]?
Paul: It is important to succeed everywhere.
BBC: The French have not made up their minds about The Beatles.

What do you think of them?
John: Oh, we like The Beatles. They're gear.

Do you like topless bathing suits?
Ringo: We've been wearing them for years.

Why don't you like Donald Duck?
Ringo: I could never understand him.

Girls rushed toward my car because it had press identification and they thought I met you. How do you explain this phenomenon?
John: You're lovely to look at.

How do you stand in the draft?
John: About five feet, 11 inches.

What about your future?
John: It looks nice.

Ringo: None of us has quite grasped what it is all about yet. But we're young. Youth is on our side. And it's youth that matters right now. I don't care about politics, just people.

George: I wouldn't do all this if I didn't like it. I wouldn't do anything I didn't want to, would I?

Paul: Security is the only thing I want. Money to do nothing with, money to have in case you wanted to do something.

John: People say we're loaded with money but by comparison with those who are supposed to talk the Queen's English that's ridiculous. We're only earning. They've got capital behind them and they're earning on top of that. The more people you meet, the more you realize it's all a class thing.

John: No more unscheduled public appearances. We've had enough. We're going to stay in our hotel except for concerts.

Won't this make you feel like caged animals?
John: No. We feed ourselves.

What did you think of Miami?
Ringo: The sun. I didn't know what it meant until I got there. But I am breathtaken to be back in England.

Were you worried about the oversized roughnecks who tried to infiltrate the airport crowd on your arrival?
Ringo: That was us.

How do you add up success?
John, Paul, George, Ringo: Money.

What will you do when Beatlemania subsides?
John: Count the money.

John: I don't suppose I think much about the future. I don't really give a damn. Though now we've made it, it would be a pity to get bombed. It's selfish but I don't care too much about humanity – I'm an escapist. Everybody's always drumming on about the future but I'm not letting it interfere with my laughs, if you see what I mean. Perhaps I was worried more when I was working it out about God.

George: Naturally I'm part of my generation. I like the way people bring things out into the open. I'd hate it if when you spoke about sex everybody curled away.

Paul: It's disturbing that people should go around blowing us up, but if an atom bomb should explode I'd say, "Oh well." No point in saying anything else, is there? People are so crackers. I know the bomb is ethically wrong but I won't go around crying. I suppose I could do something like wearing those 'Ban The Bomb' things, but it's something like religion that I don't think about. It doesn't fit in with my life.

Paul: Don't for heavens sake say we're the new youth, because that's a load of old rubbish.

Are you ever in any danger during your concerts?
Paul: I was hit once by a cigarette lighter. Clouted me right in the eye and closed my eye for the day. In Chicago a purple and yellow stuffed animal, a red rubber ball and a skipping rope were plopped up on stage. I had to kick a carton of Winston cigarettes out of the way when I played. And I saw a cigarette lighter go flying past me in Detroit's Olympia Stadium.
Don't you worry about all that?
Paul: It's OK, as long as they throw the light stuff, like paper.

Brian Epstein: That was quite a nice aircraft we flew back on.
Ringo: Let's buy it!

Do you care what the public thinks about your private lives?
Ringo: There's a woman in the United States who predicted the plane we were travelling on would crash. Now a lot of people would like to think we were scared into saying a prayer. What we did actually – we drank.

What do you think of space shots?
John: You see one, you've seen them all.

What do you think about the pamphlet calling you four Communists?
Paul: Us, Communists? Why we can't be Communists. We're the world's number one capitalists. Imagine us, Communists!

Would you ever accept a girl in your group if she would sing, play an instrument and wear the Beatle haircut?
Ringo: How tall is she?

What about the recent criticism of your lyrics?
Paul: If you start reading things into them, you might as well start singing hymns.

Beatle-licensed products have grossed millions and millions of dollars in America alone – Beatle wigs, Beatle hats, Beatle T-shirts, Beatle egg-cups, Beatlenut ice-cream . . .
Ringo: Anytime you spell Beatle with an "a" in it, we get some money.

What are your favourite programmes on American television?
Paul: News In Espanol from Miami. Popeye, Bullwinkle. All the cultural stuff.
John: I like American TV because you can get 18 stations, but you can't get a good picture on any one of them.

You were at the Playboy Club last night. What did you think of it?
Paul: The Playboy and I are just good friends.

George, is the place you were brought up a bit like Greenwich Village?
George: No. More like The Bowery.

Ringo, how do you manage to find all those parties?
Ringo: I don't know. I just end up at them.
Paul: Ringo's always out.
John: Ringo freelances.

There's a 'Stamp Out The Beatles' movement under way in Detroit. What are you going to do about it?
Paul: We're going to start a campaign to stamp out Detroit.

Who thought up the name, Beatles?
Paul: I thought of it.
Why?
Paul: Why not?

Aren't you tired of all the hocus-pocus? Wouldn't you rather sit on your fat wallets?
Paul: When we get tired we take fat vacations on our fat wallets.

Do you get much fan mail?
Ringo: We get 2,000 letters a day.
John: We're going to answer every one of them.

Do any of you have ulcers?
George: None that we've noticed.

How come you were turned back by immigration?
John: We had to be deloused.

What is your favourite food?
Ringo: I'm hung up on hamburgers.
George: All four of us are mad about hero sandwiches.
Paul: I have a yen for grilled cheese sandwiches.
John: George and I usually wait until someone else orders, then
say, "I'll have that too."

How do you feel about the invasion of your privacy all the time?
Ringo: The only time it bothers us is when they get us to the
floor and really mangle us.

*Do you worry about smoking in public? Do you think it might set a
bad example for your younger fans?*
George: We don't set examples. We smoke because we've
always smoked. Kids don't smoke because we do. They smoke
because they want to. If we changed we'd be putting on an act.
Ringo: [*whispering*] We even drink.

*What careers would you individually have chosen had you not
become entertainers?*
Ringo: A hairdresser.
George: I had a short go at being an electrician's apprentice,
but I kept blowing things up so I got dumped.
Paul: I dunno. Maybe something with art in it?

*Who in the world would The Beatles like to meet more than anyone
else?*

Ringo: The real Santa Claus.

Paul, you look like my son.
Paul: You don't look a bit like my mother.

Why aren't you wearing a hat?
George: Why aren't you wearing a tie?

Is it true that on one flight the stewardess broke up a pillow fight among you guys and got clobbered on the head?
George: I'm not really sure where she got hit. She did make us break it up though.

George: Remember that house we stayed in at Harlech?
Paul: No. Which one?
George: Yes you do! There was a woman who had a dog with no legs. She used to take it out in the morning for a slide.

Do teenagers scream at you because they are, in effect, revolting against their parents?
Paul: They've been revolting for years.
John: I've never noticed them revolting.

Do you have any special messages for the Prime Minister and your parents?
John: Hello, Alec.
George: Hello, Muddah.
Ringo: Hello, fellas.

Do you have any special message for Dutch youth?
John: Tell them to buy Beatle records.

Are you afraid military service might break up your careers?
John: No. There's no draft in England now. We're going to let you do our fighting for us.

Is your popularity beginning to taper off?

Paul: I agree that our popularity has hit a peak. But I also agreed with a man who said the same thing last year. And we were both wrong.

Do you speak French?
Paul: Non.

What's the secret of your success?
John: We have a press agent.

Is it true none of you can read and write music?
Paul: None of us can read or write music. The way we work is like, we just whistle. John will whistle at me and I'll whistle back at him.

Do you have any special advice for teenagers?
John: Don't get pimples.

How do you manage to have such a weird effect over teenagers?
George: Enthusiasm, I guess.

Did you really use four-letter words on the tourists in the Bahamas?
John: What we actually said was "Gosh".
Paul: We may have also said "Heavens!"
John: Couldn't have said that, Paul. More than four letters.

Sorry to interrupt you while you are eating but what do you think you will be doing in five years time when all this is over?
Ringo: Still eating.

What would you do if the fans got past the police lines?
George: We'd die laughing.

What will you do when the bubble bursts?
George: Take up ice hockey.
Paul: Play basketball.

HRH Prince Philip presented the awards for "The Most Outstanding Beat Group Of The Year" and "The Most Outstanding Vocal Group Of The Year" to The Beatles.

Prince Philip: Which one of you wrote the book?
John: [*raising his hand*] Me, sir.
Prince Philip: I'll swap you one of mine for one of yours.
John: Sure!
Prince Philip: You don't know what you are letting yourself in for.

How do you feel about band leader Ray Block's statement that The Beatles won't last a year?
John: We'll probably last longer than Ray Block.

How come The Beatles, rather than 200 other groups, clicked?
Ringo: Sometimes I try to figure that out too.

Why don't all four of The Beatles ever sing together?
George: Well, we try to start out together anyway.

What does each Beatle consider his two most valued possessions?
John: Our lives.

What do you do with your money?
Ringo: We bury it.
George: We hide it.
Paul: We don't see it. It goes to our office.
John: We pay a lot of taxes.

What are your feelings on the "hints of queerness" American males found in The Beatles during the early day of your climb to popularity?
Paul: There's more terror of that hint of queerness – of homosexuality – here than in England where long hair is more accepted. Our whole promotion made us look silly. But we've had a chance to talk to people since then and they can see we're not thick little kids.

Has success spoiled The Beatles?
John: Well, you don't see us running out and buying bowler hats, do you? I think we've pretty well succeeded in remaining ourselves.
Paul: The great thing about it is that you don't have big worries any more when you've got where we have – only little ones, like whether the plane is going to crash.

What is it like being The Beatles?
George: We've gotten to know each other quite well. We can stand each other better now than when we first met.

What do you plan to do after this?
Ringo: What else is there to do?

What excuse do you have for your collar-length hair?
John: Well, it just grows out yer head.

Which of you is really bald?
George: We're all bald. And I'm deaf and dumb.

Do you ever think of getting a haircut?
George: No, luv, do you?

Where did you think up the hairdos?
Paul: We got them from a German photographer who wore his hair this way.
George: It was while we were in Germany. I went in swimming and when I came out I didn't have a comb. So my hair just dried. The others liked it the way it looked and there we were.
John: We've told so many lies about it we've forgotten.

Do you wear wigs?
John: If we do, they must be the only ones with real dandruff.

How do you feel about teenagers imitating you with Beatle wigs?

John: They're not imitating us because we don't wear Beatle wigs.

Where did you get your hairstyle?
Paul: From Napoleon. And Julius Caesar too. We cut it any time we feel like it.
Ringo: We may do it now.

Are you wearing wigs or real hair?
Ringo: Hey, where's the police?
Paul: Take her out!
George: Our hair's real. What about yours, lady?

What would happen if you all switched to crewcuts?
John: It would probably be the end of the act.

Are you going to get haircuts over in America?
Ringo: What d'you mean? We got them yesterday.

Does your hair require any special attention?
John: Inattention is the main thing.

What do you look like with your hair back off your foreheads?
John: You just don't do that, mate. You feel naked if you do that, like you don't have any trousers on.

Don't you feel icky and dirty with your hair so long, flopping in your eyes and down your neck?
John: Of course not. We've got combs you know.

What is the biggest threat to your careers, the atom bomb or dandruff?
Ringo: The atom bomb. We've already got dandruff.

LED ZEPPELIN ON THEIR FOURTH LP

Jimmy Page: We started off doing some tracks at the new Island studios in London in December '70, but after that we went to our house, Headley Grange in Hampshire, a place where we frequently rehearse. For some reason, we decided to take the Stones' mobile truck there . . . because we were used to the place. It was familiar territory. We had even lived there during long rehearsal sessions. It seemed ideal – as soon as we thought of an idea, we put it down on tape. In a way, it was a good method. The only thing wrong was that we'd get so excited about an idea that we'd really rush to finish its format, to get it on tape. It was like a quick productivity thing. It was just so exciting to have all the facilities there.

Robert Plant: Most of the mood for this new album was brought about in settings that we hadn't come across before. We were living in this old falling-apart mansion, way out in the country. The mood was incredible. We could put something down on the spot and hear the results immediately. There was no waiting around until you could get into the studio.

Jimmy Page: We decided that on the fourth album we would deliberately play down the group name, and there wouldn't be any information whatsoever on the outer jacket. Names, titles and things like that do not mean a thing. What does Led Zeppelin mean? It doesn't mean a thing. What matters is our music. If we weren't playing good music, nobody would care what we called ourselves. If the music was good we could call ourselves The Cabbage and still get across to our audience. The words Led Zeppelin do not occur anywhere on this cover. And all the other usual credits are missing too. I had to talk like hell to get that done . . . the record company told us we were committing professional suicide. We said we just wanted to rely purely on the music.

The old man on the cover, carrying the wood, is in harmony with nature. He takes from nature and gives back to the land. It's a natural circle. It's right. His old cottage gets pulled down and they put him in slums – old slums, terrible places. The old man is also the Hermit of the Tarot cards – a symbol of self-reliance and mystical wisdom.

Unfortunately the negatives were a bit duff so you can't quite read an Oxfam poster on the side of a building on the back of the jacket. It's the poster where someone is lying dead on a stretcher and it says that every day someone receives relief from hunger. You can just make it out on the jacket if you've seen the poster before. But other than that, there's no writing on the jacket at all.

Robert Plant: We decided the album couldn't be called "Led Zeppelin IV" and we were wondering what it should be. Then each of us decided to go away and choose a metaphysical type symbol which somehow represented each of us individually – be it a state of mind, an opinion, or something we felt strongly about, or whatever. Then we were to come back together and present our symbols.

My symbol was drawn from sacred symbols of the ancient Mu civilisation which existed about 15,000 years ago as part of a lost continent somewhere in the Pacific Ocean between China and Mexico. All sorts of things can be tied in with Mu civilization – even the Easter Island effigies. These Mu people left stone tablets with their symbols inscribed into them all over the place . . . in Mexico, Egypt, Ethiopia, India, China and other places. And they all date from the same time period. The Chinese say these people came from the east and the Mexicans say they came from the west . . . obviously it was somewhere in between. My personal symbol does have a further meaning, and all I can suggest is that people look it up in a suitable reference work.

Jimmy Page: John Paul Jones's symbol, the second from the left, was found in a book about runes and was said to represent

133

a person who is both confident and competent, because it was difficult to draw accurately. Bonzo's came from the same book – he just picked it out because he liked it.

Robert Plant: I suppose it's (Bonzo's symbol) the trilogy – man, woman and child. I suspect it has something to do with the mainstay of all people's beliefs. At one point, though, in Pittsburgh I think, we observed that it was also the emblem of Ballantine beer.

You may not believe this, but Pagey once took me aside and said, "Look, I'm going to tell you the meaning of this once, and then I shan't ever mention it again – or at least, not for a long, long time anyway." And would you believe that I have since forgotten what it was and now Pagey won't tell me. If I know Pagey it'll turn up in some long lost book. That's the only light I can throw on it.

We were disgusted at the amount of time it had taken to get the album finished. The sound of the mixing room that Andy Johns, a producer of some note, took Jimmy to was really duff . . . Then there was a hold-up about the pressings, worrying whether they were OK or whether the masters would stand up to how many pressings.

Jimmy Page: The Battle Of Evermore . . . um, I forget whether people had gone to bed early or what, but it just came out then. I picked up John Paul Jones's mandolin, and those chords just came out. It was my first experiment with mandolin. I suppose all mandolin players would have a great laugh, 'cos it must be the standard thing to play those chords, you know, but possibly not that approach. Anyway, it was just one of those things where I was governed by the limitations of the instrument. Possibly, afterwards, it sounded like a dance-around-the-maypole number I must admit, but it wasn't purposely like that – 'Let's do a folksy number'.

Robert Plant: I'd been reading a book on the Scottish wars just before going to Headley Grange. The number (*Battle Of*

Evermore) is really more of a playlet than a song. After I wrote the lyrics, I realised that I needed another completely different voice as well as my own to give the song its full impact. So I asked Sandy Denny to come along and sing on the track. I must say I found it very satisfying to sing with someone who has a completely different style to my own. So while I sang about the events in the song, Sandy answered back as if she was the pulse of the people on the battlements. Sandy was playing the role of the town crier, urging people to throw down their weapons.

Jimmy Page: Rock'n'roll was a spontaneous combustion. We were doing something else at the time, but Bonzo played the beginning of Little Richard's Good Golly Miss Molly with the tape still running and I just started doing that part of the riff. It actually ground to a halt after about 12 bars, but it was enough to know that there was enough there as a number to keep working on it. Robert even came in singing on it straightaway.

To me, I thought Stairway crystallized the essence of the band. It had everything there and showed the band at its best – as a band, as a unit. Not talking about solos or anything, it had everything there. We were careful never to release it as a single. It was a milestone for us. Every musician wants to do something of lasting quality, something that will hold up for a long time and I guess we did it with Stairway. Townshend probably thought that he got it with Tommy. I don't know whether I have the ability to come up with more. I have to do a lot of hard work before I can get anywhere near those stages of consistent, total brilliance.

BOB DYLAN ON FAME

Would you welcome being anonymous again?
Well, I would to a degree, but not really. I wouldn't want to be anybody else except me.

I meant anonymous in the sense that you could walk down the street.
Well, yeah. Anybody would welcome that. That's another thing, but then again being me I can get all sorts of favours from people, y'know. *(1965)*

People treat famous people all the same. It doesn't matter what the person's famous for, you could be famous for the shooting of the President or something, you're still famous and they put your picture on all the newspapers. You could be a famous fashion designer or a famous movie star or a famous Wall Street executive, but you're still on your degree of fame. You know you're just famous and people react to famous people so if you talk to famous people, and I guess I am one of them because I have a certain degree of notoriety and fame, and everybody just kinda copes with it in a different way, but nobody really seems to think it's what they went after. A lot of people go after fame and money, but they're really after the money, they don't want the fame . . . It's like, say you're passing a little pub or an inn, and you look through the window and you see all the people eating and talking and carrying on, you can watch outside the window and you can see them all being very real with each other. As real as they're gonna be, because when you walk into the room it's over. You won't see them being real any more. *(1986)*

l don't pay any attention to it. I just don't. Life is too short and what do most people want? They want your autograph. Nobody knows me and I don't know them, y'know. They walk up and they think they know me because I've written some song that happens to bother them in a certain way and they

136

can't get rid of it in their mind. They got nothin' to do with me, they still don't know me and I still don't know them so they walk up as if we're long lost brothers or sisters or something. That's got nothin' to do with me. I think I could prove that in any court. *(1986)*

It wasn't me who called myself a legend. It was thrown at me by editors in the media who wanted to play around with me or have something new to tell their readers. But it stuck. It was important for me to come to the bottom of this legend thing, which has no reality at all. What's important isn't the legend but the art, the work. A person has to do whatever they are called on to do. If you try to act the legend, it's nothing but hype.

Many people describe you as a genius.
Genius? That's a real fine line between genius and insanity. Anybody will tell you that. *(1992)*

I'm not concerned with the myth, because I can't work under the myth. The myth can't write the songs. It's the blood behind the myth that creates the art. The myth don't exist for me as it may for other people. I'd rather go on, above the myth. *(1977)*

It seems funny for me to say, but I don't really care for the bright lights that much. *(1980)*

It's been years since I've read anything about myself. [People] can think what they want and let me be. You couldn't let fame get in the way of your calling. Everybody is entitled to lead a private life. Then again, God watches everybody, so there's nothing really private, there's nothing we can really hide. As long as you're exposing everything to the power that created you, people can't uncover too much. *(1979)*

Over the past 18 years or so you've been written about and analysed and criticised and second guessed and worshipped by many. As time goes on does it ever get any easier being Bob Dylan?

Well, it's easy being Bob Dylan. It's just trying to live up to what people would want Bob Dylan to do that might be difficult, but it's not really that difficult.

Is it difficult living up to those expectations? Is it something you've learned to live with, or is it a burden sometimes?
As long as I keep it straight in my mind who I am and not get that confused with who I'm supposed to be, I think I'll be all right. *(1980)*

It's important to stay away from the celebrity trap. The Andy Warhol-fame-for-a-minute type trip. The media is a great meat grinder, it's never satisfied and it must be fed but there's power in darkness too and in keeping things hidden. Look at Napoleon. Napoleon conquered Europe and nobody even knew what he looked like. People get too famous too fast these days and it destroys them. *(1985)*

Look at Elvis – he's bigger now that when he was living. He lives on in people's minds. But you wonder if people are remembering the right things about his music, rather than all the stuff people wrote about him. *(1992)*

Fame is a curse. There's a lot of truth in that.

BRUCE SPRINGSTEEN: BORN TO RUN

It's not actually a concept type thing, but it's like you get a jigsaw puzzle and you put it down on the floor and it slowly comes together. *(1975)*

It's going to feature songs around a feeling, a mood. It's going to need more instruments than the other albums to get that feel, but it can be done. *(1975)*

Here comes the third album, and I guess everybody's excited about it. My time has come, but I'm not going to count on it. I don't count on nothing. I stopped doing that a long time ago. Anything that happens now is icing on the cake. *(1975)*

I was unsure about Born To Run all the way. I didn't really know what I put down on it. I lost all perspective. The sessions turned into something I never conceived of a record turning into. It turned into this thing that was wrecking me, just pounding me into the ground. Every time you'd win a little victory over it, accomplish a little something, you'd say, "Well, the worst is over." The next day you'd come back in and it would start pounding away at you again. *(1978)*

I hated it. I couldn't stand to listen to it. I thought it was the worst piece of garbage I'd ever heard. I told Columbia I wouldn't release it. I told 'em I'd just go to the Bottom Line and do all the new songs and make it a live album. *(1978)*

I had this horrible pressure in the studio, and for the whole last part of the record, I was living in this certain inn in New York over in the West Side. And the room there had this crooked mirror and every night when I'd come home, that mirror was crooked again. Every time. That crooked mirror, it just couldn't stay straight. *(1978)*

The best thing you can say about the album is that it was the most intense experience I ever had. There was nothing ever came close. And what was worse was, like if you can imagine being at the particular height of intensity for, like, four months. Some days when you got in there it was like murder. Some of the stuff that was in the air in that studio was deadly. *(1978)*

The only concept that was around Born To Run was that I wanted to make a big record, you know, that sounds like these words. Just like a car, zoom, straight ahead, that when the sucker comes on it's like wide open. No holds barred! *(1978)*

I was going to have a song about back home on it, but I didn't get to it. There's a few oblique references but most of the songs are about being nowhere. *(1978)*

One night, towards the end of the record, I was sitting there at the piano trying to get down the last cut, She's The One, and Landau's in the booth, and we've been at it for hours and hours. I just lean my head down on the piano. It just won't come. And everyone's trying to tell me how to do it and Landau's saying this and that and freaking out and, all of a sudden, everybody looks around and Landau has just disappeared, just walked off into the night – night, it was like six am – he couldn't take it. *(1978)*

The album became a monster. It wanted everything. It just ate up everyone's life. *(1978)*

It was the weirdest thing I have ever seen. We did attempt to work on it earlier. We did the song Born To Run a year ago. And over that period, we did attempt to start the record many times. But we'd always get bogged down. Things broke. Sessions didn't work. *(1978)*

The main factor that changed things around, I guess, was Jon Landau. He was an interested party. He said, "Listen, man, you got to make an album." Like he said, I wasn't doing right by myself putting the album off as long as I did. He sort of impressed on me this fact. *(1978)*

It really dealt with faith and a searching for answers . . . I laid out a set of values. A set of ideas, intangibles like faith and hope, belief in friendship and in a better way. *(1980)*

I was born, grew old and died making the album. *(1980)*

My early albums were about being some place and what it was like there. Born To Run is about being nowhere at all. *(1980)*

It had a lot of overblown romance but it still contained the seeds of realism. *(1981)*

The one thing that bothered me about the Born To Run record was when it was initially criticised by people who thought it was a record about escape. To me, there was an aspect of that, but I always felt it was more about searching. *(1984)*

On the old stuff, there's a lot of characters and groups of people and as it goes along it thins out; people drop by the wayside, until on Born To Run, it's essentially two: it's a girl and a guy. *(1984)*

I was very doubtful of myself. You are just trying to find out about your feelings to a lot of things. *(1987)*

At the end of the record I tended to look back at it and think, "Well, it was good enough for now but these people have to go somewhere." You just can't go nowhere all the time. Basically, to have some meaning they had to be going some place. Where were these two people going? I didn't know myself. *(1987)*

All my records were a reaction to Born To Run. I asked all the questions on that album that I'm still asking today. You can't find it until you strip away the illusion. You gotta strip away the fairy tale. *(1987)*

I wanted to make a record that would sound like Phil Spector. I wanted to write words like Dylan. I wanted my guitar to sound like Duane Eddy. *(1987)*

When I was writing Born To Run, I was interested in writing bigger than life, bigger than lifesize. Lately, I've been trying to scale it down. *(1987)*

The real question in Born To Run which I asked is that I want to know if love is real. *(1987)*

FREDDIE MERCURY ON HIMSELF

I'm a man of extremes. I have a soft side and a hard side with not a lot in between. If the right person finds me I can be very vulnerable, a real baby, which is invariably when I get trodden on. But sometimes I'm hard, and when I'm strong, no-one can get to me. I'm very emotional. Whereas before, I was given time to make my decisions, now nearly all of us are so highly strung we just snap. We always argue but I think that's a healthy sign because we get to the root of the matter and squeeze the best out. But lately so much is happening, it's escalating so fast that everybody wants to know almost instantly, and I certainly get very temperamental.

You've got to know where to draw the line. But the public always come first – it's a corny thing to say but I mean it. Lately I've been throwing things around, which is very unlike me. I threw a glass at someone the other day. I think I'm going to go mad in a few years' time; I'm going to be one of those insane musicians. *(1974)*

Musicians aren't social rejects any more. If you mean "Have I got upper class parents who put a lot of money into me? Was I spoilt?" – no. My parents were very strict. I wasn't the only one, I've got a sister. I was at boarding school for nine years so I didn't see my parents that often. That background helped me a lot because it taught me to fend for myself. *(1974)*

I don't like the way my teeth protrude. I'm going to have them done, but I just haven't had the time. Apart from that . . . I'm perfect.

My nodules are still with me. I have these uncouth callouses growing in my interior (throat). From time to time they harm my vocal dexterity. At the moment, however, I am winning.

I am going easy on the red wine and the tour will be planned around my nodules. Actually, I came very near to having an operation but I didn't like the look of the doctor and I was a bit perturbed about having strange instruments forced down my throat. *(1975)*

I hate pockets in trousers. By the way, I do not wear a hose. My hose is my own. No coke bottle, nothing stuffed down there." *(1974)*

I want my privacy, and I feel I've given a lot for it. It's like Greta Garbo isn't it? Virgo, same star sign.

People are apprehensive when they meet me. They think I'm going to eat them. But underneath it all I'm quite shy. *(1976)*

I like leather. I rather fancy myself as a black panther. *(1977)*

Excess is part of my nature. Dullness is a disease. I really need danger and excitement. I've often been warned to stay away from clubs because they are too dangerous. But I revel in that – I'm never scared of putting myself out on a limb.

Money may not be able to buy happiness, but it can damn well give it!

On Queen Elizabeth II's Silver Jubilee:
The Jubilee's quite fun, isn't it? I love the Queen. I'm very patriotic. I love all this pomp, of course I do. I love it. She does outrageous things! *(1977)*

I've made no effort to become a guitar hero because I can't play the fucking guitar!

Every person who makes a lot of money has a dream he wants to carry out, and I achieved that dream with this wonderful house. Whenever I watched Hollywood movies set in plush homes with lavish decor, I wanted that for myself, and now I've got it. But to me it was much more important to get the damn thing than to actually go and live in it. Maybe the challenge has worn off now. I'm very much like that – once I get something I'm not that keen on it any more. I still love the house, but the real enjoyment is that I've achieved it. Sometimes, when I'm alone at night, I imagine that when I'm 50 I'll creep into that house as my refuge, and then I'll start making it a home. Anyway, as it is, I can only spend 60 days a year in England for tax reasons. *(1981)*

I was wearing a white scarf and holding a glass of wine when I was introduced to Prince Andrew. But I was so nervous I didn't realise my scarf was dangling in the drink. There I was trying to be really cool and suddenly the Prince said, "Freddie, I don't think you really want this getting wet." He squeezed out the scarf and broke the ice between us. I said, "Thank goodness you've put me at ease. Now I can use the odd bit of dirty language." He really got into the spirit of things and even had a dance. He's really quite hip in those sort of situations. I have a lot of respect for Royalty, I'm a tremendous patriot. *(1981)*

It's not a question of money any more. I spend money like it's nothing. You know, I could be penniless tomorrow, but I'd get back, somehow. *(1982)*

I can be very soft, very slushy and mushy. *(1983)*

If I tried that on, people would start yawning, "Oh God, here's Freddie saying he's gay because it's very trendy". *(1984)*

I like to ridicule myself. I don't take myself too seriously. I wouldn't wear these clothes if I was serious. The only thing that keeps me going is that I laugh at myself.

For God's sake, if I want to make big confessions about my sex life, would I go to The Sun, of all papers, to do it? There's no fucking way I'd do that. I'm too intelligent.

I enjoy being a bitch. I enjoy being surrounded by bitches. Boredom is the biggest disease in the world, darling. Sometimes I think there must be more to life than rushing round the world like a mad thing getting bored.

I was caught up in being a star and I thought "This is the way a star behaves". Now I don't give a damn. I want to do things my way and have fun. If all my money ended tomorrow, I'd still go about like I had lots of money because that's what I used to do before. I'll always walk around like a Persian Popinjay and no one's gonna stop me. I love living life to the full – that's my nature. Nobody tells me what to do. *(1985)*

I would have loved to have been on the Band Aid record, but I only heard about it in Germany. I don't know if they would have had me on the record anyway. I'm a bit old. *(1985)*

I never carry money, just like the real Queen. If I fancy something in a shop I always ask someone on our staff to buy it.

Darling, I'm simply dripping with money. It may be vulgar but it's wonderful! All I want from life is to make lots of money and spend it.

When I look back on all that black varnish, chiffon, satin and that, I think, God, what was I doing?

I'm a big macho, sexual object and I'm very arrogant. So most people dismiss me because of that. They don't know what I'm really like.

I can't carry on rocking the way I have done in the past. It is all too much. It's no way for a grown man to behave. I have stopped my nights of wild partying. That's not because I'm ill but down to age. I'm no spring chicken. Now I prefer to spend my time at home. It is part of growing up.

The album track Living On My Own is very me. I have to go around the world living in hotels. You can have a whole shoal of people you know looking after you, but in the end they all go away.

But, I'm not complaining. I'm living on my own time and having a boogie time.

When you're a celebrity, it's hard to approach somebody and say, "Look, I'm normal underneath". Then what happens is they tread all over me because by trying to be normal to somebody, suddenly I've come out of my shell and become far more vulnerable than most people.

Because I'm successful and have a lot of money, a lot of greedy people prey on me. But that's something I've learned to deal with. I'm riddled with scars and I just don't want any more.

I've got a few good friends, a big house and I can go wherever I want whenever I want . . . but the more money you make the more miserable you get. It just so happens that I have a lot of money.

I'm a very emotional person, a person of real extremes, and that's often destructive both to myself and others.

I love everybody, you know. I love all these beautiful brown bodies whoever they are. I think I'm a mother figure to many people. I love to share problems with people. *(In Brazil, 1985)*

PRINCE

A Documentary

Per Nilsen

Nilsen's book is unlike most of the books in this reader, being neither critical nor probing. Instead it's a fan's dream, a diary of Prince's diverse musical activities over the past decade and a half. The slivers below detail the three albums that Prince, at the zenith of his prolific creativity, made between the Springs of 1987 and '88 – the acclaimed Sign 'O' The Times, the dark and eventually suppressed Black Album and the controversial Lovesexy . . .

March 30, 1987
Sign 'O' The Times is released worldwide. Flawed and occasionally unfocused, but showcasing Prince's multifarious talents better than ever, the double LP was his most satisfying album to date. The material was less self-conscious and narcissistic than before, and the social and spiritual themes of some songs had a subdued emotional maturity lacking in most previous albums. It was argued that Sign 'O' The Times would have made a stunning single LP but it would clearly have ruined the extraordinary diversity of the material. Prince later commented:

"What people were saying about Sign 'O' The Times was 'There are some great songs on it, and there are some experiments on it.' I hate the word experiment – it sounds like something you didn't finish. Well, they have to understand that's the way to have a double album and make it interesting.

The album sold relatively poorly in the States (1.8 million

copies), reaching Number 6. Clearly, Prince had lost much of his teeny-bopper audience since Purple Rain in the States. On the other hand, he was fast becoming the darling of the critics, and attracting more loyal and devoted followers. The album sold 1.3 million copies outside of the US.

Most of the tracks were recorded by Prince on his own at Sunset Sound studios and in his home studio. Eric Leeds and Atlanta Bliss appeared on four tracks. It's Gonna Be A Beautiful Night was based on a live recording made with the Revolution in Paris (on the 1986 Parade tour). Sheila E, Lisa, Susannah and Wendy Melvoin also made guest appearances on various tracks, and Sheena Easton duetted on U Got The Look. Apart from three songs, everything was written by Prince. The lyrics of Starfish And Coffee were co-written by Susannah and the Slow Love lyrics were co-written by Carole Davis, who released her own version of the song on her 1989 debut album, Heart Of Gold. Eric Leeds and Matt Fink contributed to the music of the live-based It's Gonna Be A Beautiful Night.

Considering Sign 'O' The Times is a double album, over-indulgences are rare and it contains few fillers. Many songs contrast with the elaborate arrangements of Parade. Hot Thing, It, If I Was Your Girlfriend, Forever In My Life and the title track are all very sparsely instrumented songs, with the drum machine playing a crucial role. Other songs seem to be a reaction to the over-ambitious production of some of Parade. Songs like Starfish And Coffee, The Cross, and The Ballad Of Dorothy Parker sound like demos and give the impression of being very quickly recorded to capture on tape the mood and emotion at the time of writing.

Despite being sketchy and unfulfilled in parts, the album contains some of Prince's most impressive and coherent work. Prince reasserts his mastery of both "white" pop and rock styles and "black" funk, from the catchy pop/rock of I Could Never Take The Place Of Your Man, the innocent, charming pop of Starfish And Coffee, and the fierce and passionate rock of The Cross, to the horn-boosted funk workouts It's Gonna Be

A Beautiful Night and Housequake, possibly the funkiest number Prince has ever written. The gospel-flavoured Forever In My Life, and the stomping Strange Relationship and U Got The Look are also excellent, while the title track is a new stripped-down masterpiece in the tradition of Prince's previous skeletal songs, Kiss and When Doves Cry.

With its harsh catalogue of modern-day ills, the opening title track projects an anguished compassion in the face of the impending apocalypse:

"In France a skinny man died of a big disease with a little name, by chance his girlfriend came across a needle and soon she did the same. At home there are 17-year-old boys and their idea of fun is being in a gang called the Disciples, high on crack and totin' a machine gun."

In many ways, the song marks a new stance in Prince's outlook on life. On 1999 and Let's Go Crazy, he wanted to live for the moment and party until the end of the world, but now he wants to settle down before it's too late, a recurring theme throughout the album.

Forever In My Life is a plea for fidelity and life-long partnership, while Strange Relationship and If I Was Your Girlfriend deal with frustrating love/hate relationships. In I Could Never Take The Place Of Your Man there is a sense that love is deeper and ultimately more worthwhile than mere sex. The two ballads, Slow Love and Adore similarly convey a warmth that is largely missing from the more lascivious ballads of the past, such as Do Me Baby or International Lover.

The album received glowing reviews. Many UK and European critics felt the album was Prince's finest moment yet. Giving the album five stars out of a possible five, Q's Charles Shaar Murray raved about the album:

"Prince has both the sophistication and chops to grab some of the most tried-and-trusted elements of traditional rock, soul and R&B and, by combining and re-combining them in startlingly new juxtapositions, to place them on the line right at the cutting edge of the funk – that edge where it slices into the soft white gut of pop."

Sounds critic Robin Gibson also noted Prince's ability to borrow from other artists:

"Prince is as much consummate musical magpie as inimitable innovator and this record strikes a gorgeous balance without waltzing off into the ill-advised sound fantasies that cluttered his last two albums. A conspicuous jewel in the crown."

Highly impressed by the variety of the material, Paolo Hewitt, New Musical Express, commented on the fact that the album contained several demos:

"As with any artist of his calibre, his success rests not only with the music but the way in which that music is presented, the way in which it takes chances to further cement his self-made image as unique individual, answerable to no one. For any other artist to put out an LP which contains demos would mean the end of a career. For Prince, it only enhances a career he has so far brilliantly stage-managed."

The US reviews were somewhat less positive. Writing for Newsweek, Bill Barol felt the album lacked "the extravagant egocentricity that has occasionally marred Prince's albums", while Lenny Soute, Rock Express, said that Prince had managed to "strike an arresting balance between breathtaking innovation, luminescent musicianship and large-scale theft." Kurt Loder, Rolling Stone, called the album "dazzling," but he felt Prince could do even better, while Dennis Hunt, Los Angeles Times, said:

"Like most Prince albums, it's mainly dark, murky and sexy. Prince is too savvy to rehash material, and the new work is more soulful, sinister and definitely more obtuse than 1999. Rather than simple dance music with throwaway lyrics, it's oblique, often absorbing funk-rock."

December 7, 1987

The planned release of the Black Album is postponed. Originally to be sneaked out with a minimum of fuss and no advertising, the album, which had no title to speak of, was eventually withdrawn from release. With a plain black sleeve and only the catalogue number in peach on the spine, the album became known as the Black Album à la The Beatles' White Album.

The album contained eight tracks: Le Grind; Cindy C; Dead On It; When 2 R In Love; Bob George; Superfunkycalifragisexy; 2 Nigs United 2 West Compton; Rockhard In A Funky Place. Of these, When 2 R In Love showed up unaltered on Lovesexy, while Cat's Cindy C rap was included on an early version of Positivity, but it was dropped for the Lovesexy album.

Musically, the Black Album is very intense, containing some hard, edgy funk and rock. Le Grind, Superfunkycalifragisexy, Cindy C, and Rockhard In A Funky Place are all first-rate funky rock. The strangely titled instrumental 2 Nigs United 4 West Compton showcases frantic jazz-rock fusion. Only the soft ballad When 2 R In Love offsets the manic proceedings.

The album is full of X-rated lyrics and pornographic references. "I hate to see an erection go to waste," Prince says in Rockhard In A Funky Place, while Superfunkycalifragisexy contains the lines, "Take 'em to your crib and tie 'em to a chair and you make funny faces so they get real scared, then you turn on the neon, and you play with yourself till you turn 'em on." Dead On It is a gentle dig at rappers: "I've got a gold tooth that costs more than your house, and I got a diamond ring on four fingers, each the size of a mouse. The only good rapper is one that's dead . . . on it!"

Bob George is most startling; it features a monologue by a psychopath arguing angrily with his lady before he shoots her, "For someone who can't stand TV dinners, you sho'nuff eat enough of them muthafuckers." The harrowing tale is only alleviated by Prince's sly remark about himself, "Who does he manage? Prince? That skinny muthafucker with the high voice?"

May 10, 1988

Lovesexy, Prince's 10th album, is released. Arguably Prince's most personal and serious album, Lovesexy saw him expressing his spiritual concerns more clearly than ever before.

He presented many bold proclamations of faith and salvation. Lovesexy contrasted completely with the Black Album"s vengeful spirit, anger and dark mood. Prince described Lovesexy as "a mind trip, like a psychedelic movie. Either you went with it and had a mind-blowing experience or you didn't."

All the songs on the album were written by Prince. One song, When 2 R In Love, was originally recorded for and included on the Black Album, while Eye No was a re-working of The Ball from 1986. Prince kept the segue of "party sounds," which was originally used between The Ball and Joy In Repetition.

In the States, the cover of the album, with Prince posing demurely in the nude, in some instances received more coverage than the musical or lyrical contents. Several chain stores refused to carry the album, and Musicland Group, one of the US's largest record chain distributors, decided to sell the album but hold it behind the counter.

Even though the cover was integrally linked with the spiritual rebirth motif of the album, it generated a lot of controversy. Mavis Staples testifies that the reaction troubled Prince:

"We talked so much, especially in London when he was feeling low about Lovesexy and the reaction the cover was getting in America. It was getting him down and I told him not to let it get him down, and to remember that the people in the States aren't as broadminded as the people here."

It is possible that the controversy over the cover in the end hurt the sales of the album because it didn't sell nearly as well as expected in the States. Hardly exceeding one million copies, it was Prince's weakest selling album since 1981's Controversy. It peaked at Number 11. Sales in Europe and elsewhere were much better; it sold 1.6 million copies outside of the US, confirming Prince's growing commercial status, particularly in Europe, where the album topped the album charts in many countries, including the UK. With the exception of Purple Rain, Lovesexy became Prince's best selling album yet in most European countries.

Musically, the album is quite uncompromising in its rejection of most commercial conventions. Even though many songs on Lovesexy are highly danceable, the intricate musical textures and melodic structures, as well as the jazz-infused and often discordant horn fillings, make the music quite demanding. Many of the songs have almost too many musical ideas for their own good and threaten to sink under the weight of their arrangements.

The full-band instrumentation and complex arrangements on several songs are far removed from Prince's earlier minimalistic approach. The importance of horns also makes the music entirely different from the sparse Minneapolis sound Prince once pioneered. The arrangements of Eye No, Dance On and Lovesexy are almost too dense and riotous. Much better is Alphabet St., which is built around a syncopated percussion and a scratchy guitar. The two ballads, Anna Stesia and the falsetto-sung When 2 R In Love, as well as the simple and sweet I Wish U Heaven are other highpoints.

On Lovesexy, Prince develops some of the themes first expressed on Sign 'O' The Times. The result is a work that is both deeply spiritual and socially conscious. In the opening Eye No, Prince sees a choice between heaven and hell, between Lovesexy and Spooky Electric respectively. In his liner notes, he defines "lovesexy" as "the feeling you get when you fall in love, not with a girl or boy, but with the heavens above." Anna Stesia moves from a profession of genuine loneliness to a confirmation of God's presence. The woman, Anna Stesia, becomes a symbol for God, and he asks her, "Come to me, talk to me, ravish me, liberate my mind, tell me what you think of me, praise me, craze me, out of space and time. Maybe I could learn to love, the right way, the only way, perhaps you could show me, baby." I Wish U Heaven is a short tale of deep and abiding love based on companionship rather than sex. Prince offers a benediction to his companion: even with the relationship straining, he hopes she achieves a state of grace. Similarly, When 2 R In Love is erotic yet the lyrics are suffused with tenderness.

Two songs overtly deal with the harsh realities of living in a society which is reluctant and unable to deal with troubling issues. Prince paints a bleak picture of America in Dance On: "Little Talk Johnny blew the big score, the gang nailed his feet to a wooden floor. Nuclear ban never stays in tune, they all know the words, but the music is doomed." His solution is: "It's time for new education, the former rules don't apply, we need a power structure that breeds production instead of jacks who vandalize." Aimed at the disaffected youth of America, Positivity is a plea for positive change, "We need love and honesty, peace and harmony. Positivity, hold on to your soul." Prince ends the song with the words: "We got a long, long way to go."

The general critical opinion suggested that Lovesexy was one of Prince's strongest albums to date. Comparing it to the unreleased Black Album, Jon Pareles said in the New York Times:

"Lovesexy purveys melodies the way the Black Album knocks out rhythms. In fact, there's so much melody that Prince gets away with extraordinary liberties in his harmonies; long stretches of the album qualify as polytonal, with the rhythm section in one key and horns, keyboards and voices in others . . . While Lovesexy isn't as determinedly danceable as the Black Album, it has plenty of funky stretches. And by choosing to release Lovesexy after the near-appearance of the Black Album, Prince has let his fans glimpse the kind of choices he and other performers make routinely about image and timing."

Expectedly, many critics focused on the religious contents, some calling the album "the gospel according to Prince." Robert Hilburn, Los Angeles Times, saw the album as a musical sermon:

"There have been traces of a spiritual component in some of Prince's past songs, like God and The Cross, but they tended to be expressions of sweet surrender and devotion in the reverential tradition of gospel music . . . Much of the music is built around a radical gospel vision reminiscent of Marvin

Gaye's sex'n'salvation testimonials. If some of the songs would be welcome at a church social, there's enough R-rated imagery in others to keep the LP out of most rectory libraries."

Mark Rowland, in Musician magazine, called the music "uncompromising" and "a commercial risk". The UK reviews were mostly positive. Giving the album four and a half stars out of a possible five, Sounds' Mat Snow picked his favourite tracks in his review:

"Dance On presents a crazily skittering vision of apocalypse as grim as those of the songs 1999 or Sign 'O' The Times, quite unrelieved lyrically by the evil humour of Bob George, the killer track from the unreleased Black Album. That already legendary mystery trip shares only one number with this authorized new Prince pizza, When 2 R In Love, which harks back to his earliest slow-dance style. Alphabet St. jumps into focus as a hilarious nod to George Michael's Faith, itself an unashamed Prince steal."

SEX PISTOLS

The Inside Story

FRED & JUDY VERMOREL

The printed word has struggled to properly convey the mayhem of the Sex Pistols' short, phosphorescent, reign of terror. You had to be there, and the Vermorels were. By avoiding straightforward narrative in favour of fragmentary interviews, intertwined reminiscences and transcripts, their book comes as near as any to capturing the moment. The chunk that follows celebrates the now-infamous event that catapulted the band overnight from music press celebrity to genuine national notoriety. On December 1, 1976, the band appeared on the Today programme, a cosy, early evening ITV magazine show hosted by journalist Bill Grundy . . .

BILL GRUNDY: I'm told that the group have received £40,000 from a record company. Doesn't that seem . . . er . . . to be slightly opposed to their [deep breath] anti-materialistic view of life?
SEX PISTOL: No. The more the merrier.
BG: Really?
SP: Oh yeah.
BG: Well, tell me more then.
SP: We've fuckin' spent it, ain't we?
BG: I don't know, have you?
SP: Yeah, it's all gone.
BG: Really?
SP: Down the boozer.
BG: Really? Good Lord! Now, I want to know one thing.

SP: What?

BG: *Are you serious or are you just making me, trying to make me laugh.*

SP: No, it's gone. Gone.

BG: *Really?*

SP: Yeah.

BG: *No, but I mean about what you're doing.*

SP: Oh yeah.

BG: *You are serious?*

SP: Mmm.

BG: *Beethoven, Mozart, Bach and Brahms have all died . . .*

SP: They're all heroes of ours, ain't they.

BG: *Really? What? What were you saying, sir?*

SP: They're wonderful people.

BG: *Are they?*

SP: Oh yes! They really turn us on.

SP2: Well, they're very . . .

BG: *Well, suppose they turn other people on?*

SP [Mumbled] That's their tough shit.

BG: *It's what?*

SP: Nothing. A rude word. Next question.

BG: *No, no. What was the rude word?*

SP: Shit.

BG: *Was it really? Good heavens. You frighten me to death.*

SP: Oh, all right, Siegfried . . .

BG: *What about you girls behind . . . ?*

SP: He's like your dad, i'n'he, this geezer. Or your grandad.

BG: *. . . are you, er, are you worried, or are you just enjoying yourself?*

FAN: Enjoying myself.

BG: *Are you?*

FAN: Yeah.

BG: *Ah, that's what I thought you were doing.*

FAN: I've always wanted to meet you.

BG: *Did you really?*

FAN: Yeah.

BG: *We'll meet afterwards, shall we?*

[Laughter]
SP: You dirty sod. You dirty old man.
BG: Well, keep going chief, keep going. [Pause] Go on. You've got another five seconds. Say something outrageous.
SP: You dirty bastard.
BG: Go on, again.
SP: You dirty fucker.
BG: What a clever boy!
SP: What a fucking rotter.
[More laughter]
BG: [Turning to face camera] Well, that's it for tonight. The other rocker, Eammon, I'm saying nothing about him, will be back tomorrow. I'll be seeing you soon. I hope I'm not seeing you [to the band] again. From me though, goodnight.
[Today theme. Closing credits.]

THE PUNK ROCK HORROR SHOW
BILL GRUNDY IN FOUR-LETTER POP OUTRAGE
TV FURY AT ROCK CULT FILTH

A pop group shocked millions of viewers last night with the filthiest language heard on British television.

The Sex Pistols, leaders of the new 'punk rock' cult, hurled a string of four-letter obscenities at interviewer Bill Grundy on Thames TV's family teatime programme 'Today'.

The Thames switchboard was flooded with protests.

Nearly 200 angry viewers telephoned the Mirror. One man was so furious that he kicked in his £380 colour TV.

Lorry driver James Holmes, 47, was outraged that his eight-year-old son Lee heard the swearing . . . and kicked in the screen of his TV.

'It blew up and I was knocked backwards,' he said. 'But I was so angry and disgusted with this filth that I took a swing with my boot.

'I can swear as well as anyone, but I don't want this sort of muck coming into my home at teatime.'

159

NATURAL

Mr Holmes, of Beedfield Walk, Waltham Abbey, Essex, added: 'I am not a violent person, but I would like to have got hold of Grundy. He should be sacked for encouraging this sort of disgusting behaviour.'

But a fan of the group, girl singer Siouxsie Sue, who took part in the interview, said: 'I don't know how people can get so worked up about something that's so natural. The boys hear words like this every day.'

Lead story, Daily Mirror, December 2, 1976

GLEN MATLOCK: *[About Bill Grundy]* Oh, I think he's very clever. I don't think he was an old cunt really. It was kind of good. Who'd heard of Bill Grundy before that? He didn't mind. No matter what he said in the paper afterwards.

FOUR-LETTER PUNK ROCK GROUP IN TV STORM

Angry viewers demanded the sacking of Bill Grundy last night after four-letter words were used in his 'Today' programme. They accused Grundy of encouraging the group to use 'some of the dirtiest language ever heard on television'.

The switchboard of Thames television in London was jammed by thousands [*sic*] of calls. There were hundreds to the Daily Mail and other newspapers. One man said he was contacting his MP and others said they would complain to the Independent Broadcasting Authority. Another said he would take legal action against the TV company, the rock band and 52-year-old Grundy.

Afterwards, a duty officer at Thames said: 'Mr Grundy was very embarrassed. These people were trying to shock viewers. Everybody was flabbergasted.'

Asked later about the swearing on the programme, Grundy said: 'You'll get nothing from me so you can – off, I'm saying nothing.'

Daily Mail, December 2, 1976

SWEARING IS BANNED AT HOME, SAYS MRS GRUNDY
Mother of six, Nicky Grundy sat in the drawing room of her imposing country home yesterday and defended her husband Bill, the TV interviewer in the Punk Rock row . . .

Mrs Grundy, whose children are aged from 12 upwards, remarked: 'It's not like Bill to encourage bad language, especially at a time when children could be watching.

'I know that with the boys in the pub after a few drinks he uses some pretty strong language, but he's never allowed swearing in his own home because he hated it, and the family were never allowed to indulge.'

Daily Mail, December 2, 1976

Q: What do you think of people working in television?
STEVE JONES: Crawlers. Get in just for lots of dough and get their egos boosted by every time you see them on telly.

BIZARRE STYLE
When the group appeared – its members are celebrated for their bizarre style – the interviewer, Bill Grundy, who is not easily shocked, asked them if they would like to say something.

One parent, Mr Leslie Blunt, said: 'Our children were waiting for Crossroads when suddenly they heard every swear-word in the book. Surely a button can be pressed to stop this filthy language.'

Daily Telegraph, December 2, 1976

Q: What did you think of the Grundy interview?
MRS COOK: I thought it was wonderful. I just said: 'Oh, that's Paul.' I couldn't believe it. I said: 'That's the shirt I washed for him last week.'

TWO WEEK BAN ON GRUNDY OVER FILTHY SHOW
WERE THE PISTOLS LOADED?
PUNK ROCK GROUP 'PLIED WITH BOOZE'

TV presenter, Bill Grundy, was suspended for two weeks yesterday as a probe was started into the four-letter words used in his show.

And the row grew yesterday as it was claimed that the Punk Rock group involved, the Sex Pistols, were loaded with drink before going on the air.

Sun, December 3, 1976

Q: I'd like to hear your version of the Grundy interview.

PAUL COOK: What, how it happened?

Q: Yes.

PC: Before it happened we didn't even know we was going to go on, even on the day. We was about to set off on this tour, cos our single had just come out, and we was rehearsing in this place in Harlesden. And we got this phone call like. Malcolm said: 'Oh great, got you on the Today show.' You know, says: 'It's going to be really good. Go on there and talk about your single and that, and what's happening and going on this tour.' So this car come round and it took us to that tower wherever it is, up the West End, Euston Road. And we went in there. Didn't sort of know what was happening. Just sat around this room. There was a few of our friends there, like we had followers who were standing at the back, and we was chatting to them. We had a drink and that. Didn't get drunk, that much.

Q: How much did you have to drink, cos everyone makes out you were ...

PC: Steve had the most. He said the most. *[Laughter]* I wasn't drunk at all. I remember feeling sort of nervous of going on the

162

telly. So I was feeling very nervous at the time – I remember that. And, er, we went into this little room – I thought it was going to be a great big room cos on the telly it looks massive – and it was this little room with all these lights. And they lined us up against this wall like for the beginning of the programme. And he went straight into like: 'You've got all this money, ain't this rather against your anti-materialistic view of life?' and that, you know. Started putting us down straight away without even getting into an interview . . . *[repeats the course of the interview]* . . .

And that was it. It was all over so quick. And we just got up, just ran out laughing – like we ran straight out of the building into this car and fucked off. And the next day I couldn't believe it like. Me and Steve used to stay in Denmark Street. There was all these reporters knocking on the door like, bang bang bang bang. 'Ere what's happening?' Woke up like. 'What's happening?' you know. 'What the fuck's happening here?' 'Haven't you seen the paper?' they were going. 'Come on. What did you do? What happened?' they was going. We were going: 'What's happening?' And we looked at a couple of the papers and we couldn't believe it like. Headlines. All the press we got. For about three days, wasn't it? Non-stop.

Q: Yes, it was incredible. Everybody was talking about it.

PC: We didn't think nothing about it. I mean I forgot about it the same night, you know. I didn't think it was nothing at all. But people, they just wouldn't leave us alone after that. That was it.

AS THE MONEY ROLLS IN, ROCK GROUP FACES TOUR BAN AND TV CHIEFS SUSPEND GRUNDY. PUNK? CALL IT FILTHY LUCRE

Concerts for the Sex Pistols were cancelled and interviewer Bill Grundy was suspended last night in a row over the group's four-letter outburst on TV.

But the real four-letter word behind it was CASH. For EMI, Britain's biggest record company, has a big financial interest in the 'punk rock' men.

The firm's records chief, Mr Leslie Hill, thought the four weirdos were 'invited to be outrageous' and swear at Grundy on the Thames Today programme – and, he said, there was no question of dropping their contract. Another official admitted: 'After this row it's anyone's guess how big they could be.' But it was denied the incident was a publicity stunt.

Yet the rewards are enormous. If, as the result of the group's behaviour, a record made the Top Ten it would sell 10,000 copies a day and gross £30,000 a week with the company clearing two per cent on every single.

. . . the group was signed in September for £40,000 by Nick Mobbs for EMI and its first record was released last week . . .

At this critical time the strength and influence of EMI's promotion and marketing ensured a series of remarkable appearances for a brand-new group – on London Weekend's London Programme, BBC TV's Nationwide, BBC Radio Four and Newsbeat, and finally, of course, Thames TV, in which EMI has a 50 per cent share.

Daily Express, December 3, 1976

Q: I would like to ask you about the fact that EMI as a company does have links with Thames Television. It owns a considerable amount of shares in it, and one newspaper in particular raised the issue that it wasn't exactly against EMI's interests to have somehow got the Sex Pistols on to the Grundy show, and then perhaps the thing went too far. But it could really have paid off. In fact, maybe it did pay off in terms of giving them a vast amount of publicity which they wouldn't have had before and maybe a publicity that wasn't really warranted by the stage that they had arrived at; I mean they were a very small concern at that time.

LAURIE HALL (*Business Affairs Manager, EMI*): Yes, I must say that Thames Television is an associate company of EMI

Limited and is associated to EMI Records, but what happened on Thames TV was in no way contrived or planned by EMI and in fact EMI Records has no control over what Thames Television does at all. It just happened. It wasn't planned at all.

Q: How was the initial contact made? Did you contact the Today programme and suggest that they might like to consider having the Pistols on the programme?

LH: I don't know exactly. Undoubtedly it's our job in the promotion of any group to get them as much exposure in the media as possible, and I would imagine that when the possibility arose of them appearing on the Today programme we were obviously behind it; remembering at that time we didn't know at all what was going to happen. Yes, I would think we – we must have been to a lesser or greater extent instrumental in getting them on TV, as we are with any group – any publicity of this sort is good.

MICHAEL HOUSEGO (*Today studio producer*): . . . the object of this particular item was to find out why people put safety pins through their noses; the same as if I'd been here 20 years ago I'd want to know why people wore drainpipe trousers and had Tony Curtis haircuts or latterly why mods and rockers punched the shit out of one another on Brighton beach . . . *[Concerning the 'top level probe']* . . . nothing happened that night really except we went to see Jeremy and John [*bosses*] together and had a discussion. Then we dealt with phone calls nearly all night, and press. The next day – no, the next evening – I was called in, and I went in with Lew Gardner, who was then our father of the chapel in the NUJ, and I was given an official reprimand but not on my record; and the same happened to Tom Steel... I mean if you go and find my file in personnel, it will not say: 'Put Sex Pistols on' . . . 'bad research, should have known . . . I didn't even get a free album of the Sex Pistols. To this day *[laughing]* I've never had a free record from the Sex Pistols. Speaking with my television hat on, it was a bit embarrassing . . . Well, I'm not the sort of person who likes to be on the front page. I like to write front pages, not be in 'em.

TONY BULLEY [*Today director*]: Especially for such a shabby and inconsequential item.

JOHN PEEL: I was really frankly appalled [by the Grundy incident] because if you took any four or five lads off the street, 17, 18, 19, 20-year-old lads, made them feel important and filled them full of beer and put them on television and said to them, 'Say something outrageous,' they'd say something outrageous. I rather suspect that – as a middle-class individual of 38 – if they did the same to me, I'd do the same. So for those people then to wring their hands in horror and say, 'This is outrageous,' is just bare-faced hypocrisy, I think, and it's shocking. I was really outraged about that.

CATCH A FIRE

The Life Of Bob Marley

TIMOTHY WHITE

**Named after The Wailers' first widely available LP,
Catch A Fire is a benchmark music biography.
By combining his close contacts with the artist
and painstaking general research, Timothy White
succeeds in telling Bob Marley's remarkable life
story, while putting the third world's first, and so far
only, superstar into a perspective that's as much
historical and political as it is musical.
The passages extracted here, however, spotlight
Marley's distinctly unusual domestic arrangements.
It's the mid-'70s; The Wailers are establishing a
worldwide reputation and Island Records boss Chris
Blackwell has just bought a large wooden mansion
on one of Kingston's most desirable boulevards. It
was to become the pivotal location of
Bob Marley's life . . .**

IN THE EARLY 1970s, Chris Blackwell bought a run-down great
house at 56 Hope Road in uptown Kingston. It was a two-
storey jalousied building set back from the road behind rusty
iron gates. In back of the main building were several acres of
property bisected by a rambling succession of shacks, sheds
and decrepit carriage houses.

The palatially shabby complex was just down the street from
both the prime minister's residence and Devon House, a
showpiece of colonial architecture built in 1881 by a millionaire
who had made his bucks in South America. Now an official

landmark, Devon House was the preferred site for fashion shows and "ethnic dance concerts" sponsored by the society ladies of St. Andrew.

Blackwell's new address, renamed Island House, was the command post for his expanding reggae interests in Kingston. It was also an attempt to put down some new roots of his own in Jamaica. When the Terra Nova had been sold in 1960, his mother retreated to Bolt House, a North Coast mansion built on a sweeping lawn overlooking the sea in Port Maria. Blanche Blackwell had also let go of the family's summer retreat in the Blue Mountains – a large hilltop cottage in an area called Greenwich, not far from Newcastle, an old cliffside fort high in the mists where the Jamaica Defence forces trained, and Red Light, the village where the off-duty soldiers did their whoring.

Although the record business had been good to him, Chris was in need of personal renewal, having been through an unsuccessful marriage with Josephine Hyman, the wealthy ex-wife of one of his best friends, David Hyman. And then there had been an extended affair with Esther Anderson, a beautiful mulatto Jamaican film actress from the village of Esher, St. Mary's. The daughter of an East Indian mother and a prominent white Jamaican architect, Esther had starred in such British films as The Touchables (1968), and had just completed shooting on A Warm December, playing opposite Sidney Poitier, who also directed the film.

Besides being prime real estate, Island House was a sentimental choice for a new base in uptown Kingston, since it was just a five-minute drive from the Terra Nova. And to compensate for the loss of the beloved retreat in Greenwich, Chris had Strawberry Hill, a rambling estate in the Blue Mountains which was perched on a knoll midway between Irish Town (where the retired Bustamante lived) and Newcastle. From the back porch of the run-down planter's house in the centre of the grounds, he could glimpse the old cottage through the slow-drifting cloud cover.

Bob had begun to frequent Island House late in 1972 and was plainly covetous of the place. Surprisingly, Blackwell seemed to enjoy this. By the time Catch A Fire was released, Bob had made a deal with Blackwell whereby he would eventually take over the property so that he would have a proper address at which to meet and greet the press. He moved in with several dread brethren and Lee Jaffe, a white American musician-filmmaker who had met Bob in New York City through Jim Capaldi of Traffic. Lee and Bob had hit it off immediately and travelled down to Carnival in Trinidad on a chartered DC-3 with Chris Blackwell, Esther and Capaldi. Bob and Lee wrote a nonsense song together called Trinidad, We Don't Like Your Carnival, when they discovered the scarcity of ganja during the rum-drenched celebration. Esther was amused by Lee and rather taken with Bob, and eventually joined them at Hope Road.

Word spread around Trench Town that the Tuff Gong had moved to a big white house uptown, but nobody would believe it. A contingent of dreads went up to check for themselves one morning, and when they saw Bob sitting on the veranda strumming his guitar, some white woman massaging his shoulders, they got "bringly" (irritated) *ta raas* and commenced vexing something fierce. Bob had to go down to Rema and explain himself. He got a fairly cool reception when he told the gang that his house was theirs too, and that they were free to come and go as they pleased. But the brethren didn't especially feature walking four miles just to "rest I head" in the courtyard of some long-dead slave driver's old digs. And if they did make the trek, they often found that all the shady places in the grounds were already taken by Bob's new friends. No one could puzzle out how he had made so many new acquaintances so swiftly. But there they were – fancy-looking women in designer jeans and silk blouses, white guys with British accents and gold cigarette lighters, brown dudes poppin' style in aviator shades and $40 slacks that they couldn't possibly have purchased in Kingston. Bob explained that they all worked for the record company and most of them split at the end of the day. The Rema crowd figured that was cool – sorta.

Bob and Rita were raising a family. Cedella had been born in 1967, David in 1968. Bob said he wanted to "'ave as many child as dere were shells on de beach". (The beach they went to nowadays was the one at Bull Bay, located about six miles outside of Kingston.)

Bob was a quality Rastaman now, committed to good health and an ital life-style that stressed a daily regime of exercise. He liked to rise before the sun, asking his ghetto buddy Antonio "Gilly" Gilbert, who was also his resident ital cook, to fix him a cup of bush tea, either mint or cerasee (a seeded vine that when boiled produces a bitter tea said to be good for clearing the blood). After that he'd roll a sleek spliff, take up his guitar and put out a nice vibe, and then begin "ta work fe stamina".

His many companions in these activities, besides Lee, Esther and Gilly, included Bunny and a new breddah named Alan "Skill" Cole. Gilly was a respected local soccer player, often called "General G'wan" or "Stonewall Jackson" because of his no-nonsense ball handling. Alan, on the other hand, was a professional footballer and coach of international renown – on a par, some said, with Pele – and the only dread on the heavyweight soccer circuit when Bob first checked fe him.

A close, even symbiotic relationship had existed between Jamaican footballers, musicians and gunmen for as far back as the ghetto brethren could recall. But there had never been so prestigious and powerful a combination as Skilly Cole and Bob Marley, and the gunmen involved in the violent political tug-of-war between the JLP and the PNP that was being called "Heavy Manners" and the "Final Battle For Jamaica" completed an awesome, unholy trinity. There is a sphinx in Egyptian mythology from which the Greeks fashioned the composite beast they called Chimera. The ghastly creature had a lion's head, a goat's body and a serpent's tail. Bob was the lion in the Jamaican Chimera, Skilly the kicking goat, the gunmen the nested snakes.

The routine was always the same: everybody would try to get up in the morning before Bob, but no one ever did. Some would attempt to outlast him the night before, but that never worked either. It was uncanny; Bob was always the last to take to his little mattress in his upstairs bedroom (bare except for a portrait of Selassie hanging on the wall) and the first to awake. If everybody passed out around 3am, Bob was asleep at 3.15; if one of the dreads lasted until first light, Bob did too. If Bob had to miss his sleep entirely to maintain the upper hand, he did and seemed none the worse for wear.

From 1973 on, the elite dread crew around Hope Road consisted of Bunny; Alan "Skilly" Cole; Antonio "Gilly" Gilbert; Neville Garrick, a graduate of the UCLA College Of Fine Arts (and disciple of Angela Davis) who had returned to Jamaica in 1973 to be an art director for the Jamaica Daily News, but met Bob and became Tuff Gong Records' resident designer; Bird, a soft-spoken ghetto breddah of Bob's; the Wailers band. Others included Lee Jaffe, Alvin "Seeco" Patterson and keyboard player Earl "Wire" Lindo, another Kingstonian; Rita and the kids; Diane Jobson, Bob's lawyer and confidante; ravishing model Cindy Breakspeare; Virginia Burke, who was a friend of Cindy's from London; Esther Anderson; guitarist Ben "Sticko" Mitchell, Bob's informal male secretary; Lips, his sometime bodyguard; assorted dreads from shantytown just passing through to draw on the chillum, plus a steady trickle of attractive young women, most of whom were known only by their first names, but a few, like Lucien Pounder and Yvette Morris-Anderson (no relation to Rita or Esther), were treated with greater deference because of their closeness to Bob.

Peter Tosh visited occasionally with his girlfriend, Evonne. Chris Blackwell was constantly in and out, sometimes with his second wife, the former Marilyn Richards, or with his best friend, Dickie Jobson (Diane's brother), who was the sometime manager of the Wailers. Increasingly, Chris either stayed at one of the two hotels (the Kingston Sheraton and the Pegasus) in the fenced-in, guard dog-patrolled New Kingston tourist compound or at remote Strawberry Hill.

Regardless of the previous night's activities (which always centred on smoking herb, singing songs and discussing

Selassie), Bob, Bunny, Skilly, Sticko, Lips, Gilly and Bird would be ready at sunrise for a jog, usually on the sprawling Jamaica House grounds near the police officers' club or at the field site of the Water Commission near Hope Road. But this was merely an "open-yeyes" sprint. If Bob was in the mood "fe discipline in stamina", then everybody would follow as he led the way along Hope Road and down Mountain View Avenue on to Windward Road, heading in the direction of the airport. At the traffic circle, the group would hook a right, and move out, running abreast along the Palisadoes peninsula, for as long as anyone could stand it.

On Sundays, the jogging entourage might go the whole eighteen-odd miles to Port Royal Point, their lengthening locks dancing in the wind. If they hadn't arranged for a car to pick them up, they'd hike back and pile into Bob's car for a drive to Bull Bay, where they'd wash themselves in the Cane River Falls, scrubbing each other's locks, and then position themselves in the roaring falls so that the torrents pounded against their chests and backs. Next they'd ride to Papine Market, and Gilly would select the day's produce: calaloo, pop-chow (a Chinese vegetable akin to Swiss chard), okra, yams, mangoes, citrus, bananas, plantains, gungo peas, rice, sweet potatoes, guava, pawpaw (papaya), cassava, breadfruit, ackee, arrowroot, avocado. Gilly would also purchase some snapper, kingfish, goatfish and doctor fish. For juices, Bob himself would choose the carrots, soursop and Irish moss, a type of seaweed used for making a sweet, gelatinous drink believed to encourage the libido. ("It mek yuh cum taste sweet, yahso!" according to Bob). Everything would be stuffed into the car and taken back to Hope Road, where Gilly would prepare for a communal "ninyam" (meal). If they were feeling "ninyam-surrey" (hungry enough to devour the whole county of Surrey), he'd prepare an ital feast, the consumption of which would take up most of the rest of the day.

If the band wasn't recording or rehearsing, everyone just milled around the Hope Road complex until Bob organized the afternoon soccer game. If there weren't enough breddahs on hand for two full teams, the game took place informally on the front lawn at Hope Road. Conventional 11-against-11 matches were played on the Boy's Town field or on the police depot grounds in Rae Town. Bob played inside right and was a strong darter and dribbler who preferred passing over shooting; he left the scoring to Alan, whom he idolized. Cole was a native of East Kingston who had left his roots there years before to play for the Boy's Town team in West Kingston – a very controversial move in a city that takes both neighbourhood loyalties and football quite seriously. In the early 1970s he had gone to Brazil to play, and then returned to lead the Jamaica Santos team. When he and Bob got chummy, the entire country took notice, their "football friendship" imitated by many boys in the ghetto, who referred to their own best buddies (à la Mutt and Jeff) as "Gong" or "Skilly".

The early Hope Road scene could be described as a non-dogmatic religious hippie commune, with an abundance of food, herb, children, music and casual sex. Jamaica being a country with a small but obsessively ambitious middle class, the American hippie movement did not arrive on the island for quite some time. It was not until well-to-do, hardcore hippie vagabonds who had survived the late 1960s began to make their way to ready-made paradises like Maui, St. Martin, St. Bart's and other tropical islands in the early 1970s that they discovered Jamaica. These tanned young haves who masqueraded as have-nots established beachheads and campsites between Port Maria and Port Antonio on the North Coast, and in the Chicken Lavish area of Negril, which was adjacent to Bloody Bay and Long Bay on the South Coast.

There seemed to be a superficial affinity between rich hippies and Rastas, the former having inherited the means to turn their backs on much of society, the latter having inherited the conviction. The Rastaman knew he had no choice; the hippies, full of themselves, said the same thing as they sat half-naked on the patio at Rick's Café and sipped rum punch. Young middle- and upper-class Jamaicans were drawn to these hot spots and happenings, and they began to mimic the appearance of Rastas – but they completely disregarded the strict dietary rules, the religious beliefs and the humility of the authentic dreads. Rude boys did likewise. Eventually, these two groups of quasi-dreads began to trip on acid, share the rum bottle, sprinkle opium into their spliffs and cruise the hippie strongholds in search of various kinds of action.

Jamaica had been trying to shake off the Caribbean malaise and establish itself in the world community since the days of Norman Manley and Bustamante. To this end, the government had undertaken a highly aggressive tourist campaign in the late 1960s, hoping to lure businessmen who would want to hold sales conferences at the island's hotels, purchase land along its coasts, and invite other investors and real estate speculators to help develop a poor but beautiful island that was not plagued with the population density and dictatorial oppression of other island nations in the area.

But these promotional campaigns succeeded mostly in attracting American hippies, who in turn were discovering and celebrating the *last* aspect of Jamaican culture the government wanted to promote: the Rastafarians – a murky, mystical cult composed of sufferahs who were praying every day for the whole island to sink into the sea in a hail of fire and brimstone, while the rest of the population was praying for Tappan ranges, colour TV and young doctors and lawyers who would marry their sons and daughters.

THE LIFE OF JIMI HENDRIX

'Scuse Me While I Kiss The Sky

DAVID HENDERSON

**Greil Marcus, doyen of rock writers, has called
Henderson's book "the strongest and most
ambitious biography yet written about any
rock'n'roll performer". Simple as that. In this
extract, the nascent guitar genius arrives in London
and manager Chas Chandler activates the plan that
would see his charge propelled from obscurity
to superstardom . . .**

THEY ARRIVED IN England on September 21, 1966. Midway
across the Atlantic, Jimmy James had become Jimi Hendrix.
Chas Chandler immediately took "Jimi" round to British blues
man Zoot Money's house where he was, in effect, greeted with
a jam.

The English authorities denied Hendrix a work permit. The
best they could do was a five-day visa. Chas Chandler had to
move quickly. He was about to launch a star – a star on a par
with Bob Dylan, The Beatles, The Rolling Stones – and would
accept nothing less.

The jam got word moving through the grapevine. Through
transatlantic calls from the States and now during the first few
days in London, Chandler made sure that his contacts were
well informed as to who Jimi was, what they intended to do,
and that they intended to succeed.

Chandler knew better than to allow Hendrix to ponder their
hazardous course. Hendrix for his part was so gassed to be in
England that he indulged in sightseeing as if he were a tourist.

It was essential that they get the band together right away. Hendrix solved a lot of the problems of band members himself. He was able to play so much guitar that they would need only the barest number of sidemen; in fact, two: a drummer and a bass player.

Linda Keith spread the word as well, especially among the ladies. Hendrix was a treat they deliciously anticipated.

Working papers were another problem – a big problem. They had to convince the authorities that Hendrix possessed a talent that could not be duplicated by any working or idle Englishman. The music people did not have to be convinced; the government authorities did.

They rushed to get it together. When Chas Chandler called for bass players and drummers to audition, many quite naturally felt that they were auditioning for The Animals. When they saw Jimi that thought quickly disappeared – The Animals were not likely to change their style for this American black, and change they would have to, because this black dude was quite something else.

Noel Redding was chosen largely because of the way he looked. Bouffant frizzly red Caucasoid-Afro hair, framing a sensitive and intelligent face. He would be receptive. Primarily a guitarist with the fluidity of a guitarist, he became a bass player immediately upon meeting Hendrix. Actually it was a lucky stroke. They had had a lot of trouble finding a bass player. Hendrix knew what he wanted. And what he wanted there was no model for. It had become apparent that playing with Hendrix was not easy. Hendrix, an excellent bass player himself, was able to tell Noel Redding exactly what to play. Noel Redding, having never played the bass before, had only to follow his lead. He looked right, he acted right, and played what he was told. Perfect.

Mitch Mitchell, on the other hand, was cocky, brash, and very confident of his abilities on drums. A typical drummer's attitude. He had played with the best of jazz and rock bands in England and was a jazz enthusiast as well. Unable to hide a strange contempt for Jimi, he channelled it into his playing, where he more than kept up; he challenged. He provided a driving tension that never let up – even beyond performance.

The Jimi Hendrix Experience was born October 12, 1966. Once the group was decided upon – Jimi Hendrix, Noel Redding, and Mitch Mitchell – Chas Chandler began his plans to four-wall them in all the hip clubs in London. Special showcases, as opposed to duration runs with several sets per night, were preferred. Mini-concerts from the onset. From the beginning the message of this phenomenon was: This is a special act. The hip, the intelligent, the connoisseur take heed. This is a very special talent being handled in a very special way. But Chandler knew that nothing would really happen without a record.

On October 15, 1966, Jimi sat in with Brian Auger and the Oblivion Express at Blaises Club. At once there was a quick flurry of success. They were spotted by *the* Johnny Halliday, the hottest singer on the Continent, who flew them to Paris to appear with him in a tremendous show he was headlining at the Olympia on October 18, 1966. It was sold out; 14,500 in the audience saw the fresh, newly established Experience, who had not played together a month. They played rhythm and blues standards Midnight Hour and Land Of A Thousand Dances, Respect, and also Everybody Needs Somebody To Love – they tore the house up – the French fans loved them.

The Jimi Hendrix Experience's first gig in London was on the same bill with Cream at Central Polytechnic. Next they appeared on the popular TV show Ready, Steady, Go! where they debuted Hey Joe, their first single recording.

The showcases came after that, The Marquee, The Court of St. James's, Blaises, The Upper Cut. Linda Keith was always in evidence with a bevy of guests, mainly young and important women, with their old men in tow. Hendrix was an immediate happening in the underground, the "in" crowd. But then there was the rest of the people who had to be convinced, especially the recording companies.

Chandler carefully nurtured the local recording deal. The advance would be nothing as compared with America – but it would mean solid finance. A chance to recoup and then really get out there.

While the initial press was great – a smash in Paris, a smash in Soho, a smash in the underground (which, it seems, had been waiting for the Experience) – the smash with the "money" was another story. The English did not quite know what to make of this black phenomenon. The press began to ridicule him: Fleet Street stuck Hendrix with the label "The Wild Man Of Pop". Could he withstand the viciousness of the establishment press? Could the London underground, which was just emerging itself, successfully champion Hendrix? The money was standing back, seeing what would transpire. Chas Chandler decided to fight. Fire with fire. He encouraged the establishment press to ridicule Hendrix. The more outrageous Hendrix would appear in the Daily Mirror, the more the rebellious youth would side with him. The question was, when would they eventually make that catalyst work?

And once the Fleet Street papers got a good look, they made him the perfect anti-hero. One London paper called him a "Mau-Mau" in banner headlines, another called him a "Wild Man from Borneo". Jimi Hendrix was denounced by Mary Whitehouse, leader of the National Viewers' And Listeners' Association. Donald Bruce wrote in Pop Shop: "For one thing, Jimi is scarcely likely to qualify for a best-looking-bloke competition." And in boldface type: "So why should Jimi worry if he looks like a wild-eyed revolutionary from the Caribbean and that he talks with the shuteye still in his big mouth?"

The youth, the first generation stripped of England's vast colonial wealth, had to deal with the hard facts of a lower standard of living. The press made sure they knew this. The underground was an important vanguard, but very small in actual numbers. The major youth divisions were the Mods and the Rockers. A press invention based on upper-middle-class and lower-middle-class youths. The Skinheads, the rowdy working-class kids, were considered out of it. They dug reggae and violence. They even took to hanging out with the West Indian rude boys in the reggae clubs.

But few English youths could escape the traditional hatred of blacks, even Noel Redding and Mitch Mitchell.

The incongruity of these young fey Englishmen having taken up with "The Wild Man of Pop" did even more to project Hendrix's image in the United Kingdom. While this cooled out some of the hostility he might have received (the group was two-thirds home-bred), it also was outrageous theatre. Noel and Mitch, both sporting the early John Lennon short German cut when they started with Jimi, soon affected long and wild hair.

Rather staid young Englishmen, both Mitchell and Redding dug jazz and blues (as any English musician did who wanted to be heavy in the pop world), and both wanted badly to make it. Before Jimi they had never become tight with a black man, and especially never considered one their superior. Although the money increased, and all the side benefits were good, Noel and Mitch found it difficult to ignore the fact that they were second to Hendrix.

The circumstance of their hiring (like a hiring hall scene) notwithstanding, Noel and Mitch began to challenge Jimi personally and in the press about their lack of prestige in the Experience. Jimi made many placating statements to the English press, but the conflict persisted. Both Mitchell and Redding were no newcomers to "pop" music. Mitchell had played with several popular and respected groups, his last being Georgie Fame's Blue Flames. Noel Redding had played with The Loving Kind.

Noel and Mitch would sometimes use racial slurs when they talked. They would use "nigger" and "coon" in banter, but it must have had an effect on Jimi and further increased the conflict among them.

Up on the stage, the conflict assumed different proportions. They openly challenged Hendrix at every juncture – playing their young asses off – and that's exactly what Hendrix wanted. Redding, who considered himself primarily a guitarist, burned up the bass line, often tuned to full volume, pushing Hendrix as far as he could. Virtuoso Hendrix seemed to revel to go higher in the fire.

179

Mitch Mitchell played every rhythm possible, extending from simple timekeeping all the way to Elvin Jones's circular rhythm jazz drumming. Noel Redding, his bass guitar often jacked up to the highest treble intensity, seemed to vie with Jimi's lead guitar and vocals. This energy, fuelled by class and colour conflict, gave the Experience the full-range sound Hendrix wanted.

By 1966-67, The Beatles had already established their worldwide fame. Taking a chance that paid off big, they began writing and performing songs with more English flavour; very much away from international pop, with its strong dose of Chuck Berry rockabilly rhythm and blues, which had made them until that point. The Beatles, in terms of class-conscious London society, had achieved aristocracy (at least on paper), while The Rolling Stones were yet to emerge as a number one supergroup. The Stones had hit after hit but were still strongly into the blues idiom. The Stones (with the exception of Brian Jones) looked on Hendrix's emergence with consternation, as did Eric Clapton and Peter Townshend of The Who.

Hendrix had pressed the English music world to the wall, thus precipitating a brief debate over how they should react. While the English authorities put Hendrix through the mill, the English rock world got it together much quicker. Townshend and Clapton conferred, as did the Stones and The Beatles – truth won out: Hendrix's music *was* unique and powerful, and his act was outasight. More importantly, Hendrix did not have a name in the States at all, aside from being known as a good traditional R&B guitarist. So why not accept him? Make him their own, and lend even more power and veracity to English rock. They were right. Hendrix, as an English commodity, took over where The Beatles left off, and gave English music the strongest dose of real black music it had ever had.

One of Chas Chandler's first moves with Hendrix was to insulate him in the word-passing in-group of English rock masterminds: Les Perrin, Derek Taylor, Brian Epstein, Andrew Loog Oldham, and – for the crucial money at the crucial juncture – his partner Michael Jeffery.

The first party Jimi went to in London blew his mind. Everyone there looked and talked like English royalty, like they were heirs to the throne. Jimi just sat in a corner cross-legged on the floor and took everything in. He was unsure of what would happen in the future there, and the hip set was still unsure as to whether they would accept him.

Marianne Faithfull had just begun to live with Mick Jagger when Jimi Hendrix first appeared in London, but she was well aware of his arrival. Not only had Linda Keith informed her, but also there had been talk of an audition that Hendrix had done for Mick, who was establishing his own production company at the time. Although Jagger had rejected Hendrix, the London hip society of musicians very much was taken with him. Brian Jones raved about Hendrix. Some took that as a signal of the widening rift between Jones and Jagger, but there were others, like Eric Clapton and John Mayall, whose words of awe could hardly be disputed.

Marianne and Mick had attended the opening of a new club, the 7½, and Hendrix had played. Jagger, as "King of the Scene", as John Lennon had dubbed him, had gone primarily out of a sense of duty. This was one of Marianne and Mick's first appearances in public and they had not stayed long. There was still the stigma of Chrissie Shrimpton's attempted suicide hanging over Jagger, and they had not wanted it to look as if they were flaunting anything. But they did want to establish their relationship in the eyes of the public and their peers.

Marianne was intrigued by what little she had heard of Jimi's playing. She had never before heard anyone play in his style, with his speed and apparent root knowledge of the blues.

A couple of days later, Hendrix reappeared at the 7½ Club for a three-day gig. Marianne had been killing time while Mick was in the studio recording. She decided to go have an anonymous drink at the club. Although there were several empty tables, the atmosphere was charged with excitement. She sat on the floor through the set enthralled. She returned the next night. She felt some kind of bond between herself and

Hendrix. It was something impossible to put into words. She felt drawn to him in a special way. Not particularly sexual, the attraction was more like a mutual recognition of each other's soul. That second night they were introduced. She knew it would be impossible not to be recognized and now that they were staring at each other she affirmed their affinity.

Jimi was very polite, as usual, but he was also coming on to her. She was used to being come on to. She was attractive, famous, upper-class, and well-to-do. Sometimes men came on to her because they felt they were supposed to. As if there was some kind of propriety her beauty demanded that made it the thing to do. Jimi came on to her rather strongly. If it had not been for the affinity she felt they shared she might have been taken aback. But she took it as a recognition on his part that they had something strongly in common. She, too, wanted to affirm the feeling. She did not necessarily want to go to bed with Jimi. She had only been living with Jagger a few weeks; they were very happy and very turned on to each other. At another time in her life it might have been a beautiful thing to do, but that night it could not happen. Instead, she asked Jimi if he might like to come to a get-together. She would invite some of her friends and they would hang out after the gig, get high, and talk. Although it was a substitution or a sublimation, it was also an affirmation.

Brian Jones came. He was not too involved in the latest sessions the Stones were doing. They were laying tracks. He would come in later and add touches and whatnot (although it seemed as if he were being frozen into that role – further and further away from ever contributing songs to the Stones' effort). Linda Keith attended, as did Paul McCartney, Chas Chandler, and some young socialites. It was no big thing. They sat around and smoked and got acquainted. There were others there, Mitch and Noel not knowing quite how to act, and Kathy Etchingham, who appeared to be Jimi's old lady, although he seemed to have eyes only for the blonde and delicately featured Marianne. They had a nice low-keyed time, but Jimi had seemed somewhat disappointed, although his shyness made some of his emotions ambiguous. Marianne was firmly with Mick, there was no disputing that. But she was glad she and Jimi had had a chance to get together and chat. For Jimi it was almost like having tea, at two o'clock in the morning.

Hey Joe had been a song that Chas and Jimi had agreed upon almost by telepathy even before they had left the States for London. It expressed a simple, emotional defiance of authority through a tale of a crime of passion. A perfect vehicle for Jimi's husky-toned voice, Hey Joe also had a feel to it that they were both confident of. It didn't really showcase Jimi's guitar as much as they would have liked, but it was a rather safe vehicle for the London market.

> Hey Joe, where ya going with that gun in your hand?
> I'm going out to shoot my ol' lady
> I caught her making love with another man

The lines would have been impossible to sing legato, but Jimi's slurring rap placed the ballad perfectly in the minds of the listeners. Not only could they visualize the scene, but they could also relate – like Frankie And Johnny, the theme was universal.

The bridge was the hippiest thing happening musically. Jimi and Noel dubbing long bass runs. Jimi's rhythm licks were subtle but effective, giving a hint of his virtuosity without taking away from the song as a whole.

Jimi's vocal uses two voices, the voice of Joe and the voice of a commentator. But the last voice in the song is Joe's as he flees South to Mexico, where no hangman will put a noose around his neck. Jimi gets a chance to take the song to another level, shouting and emoting as the song slowly fades.

Edwin Kramer, slight, blond-haired young engineer, had just started on his new job at Olympic Studios when in walked Jimi Hendrix – the most incredible electric guitarist in England.

Chas and Jimi were not satisfied with the Hey Joe recording they had made at another studio. They wanted to feature Jimi's guitar work more, but the more way-out stuff was difficult to record. At this point they knew that an amount of experimentation would have to take place in order to get the recorded sound they wanted. They had had their fill of the staid middle-aged engineers. They liked Kramer from the beginning. He was different, young, and enthusiastic. He would be willing to put in the extra time and effort, as opposed to the company men who freaked out when it was past tea-time and they were still in the studio. Besides, Kramer looked like an angel, a cherub, a cupid. His vibes were right.

It would be a job just to get what Jimi did on stage on a four-track tape in the studio. But they wanted more than that. They wanted to *extend* his sound via magnetic tape. They wanted the best recordings and then some. What Jimi was hearing would involve elaborate overdubbing and the most advanced devices to deliver both his quick picking and his distortion and feedback harmonics. But the total Experience sound needed something more as well. The bass had to have absolute depth without distortion in the small speakers common to radio. The drums also needed a boost in order to feature their dynamic interplay with Jimi's lead. With only four-track machines to work with, Hendrix's music was a problem. Kramer took Hey Joe home with him and played it all night. The next day he had some ideas and suggestions. That really sold Chas and Jimi. Edwin worked like an elf.

The Jimi Hendrix Experience's first gig at the Olympia in Paris had been grander than they could ever have hoped for. It was a good sign, an august beginning. But Chas Chandler knew that it was necessary to deal with London – and that no matter how much they had going for them it was still going to be an uphill battle. While the JHE recorded at a frantic pace, Chas was talking record deals. Chas and Jimi would frequent the hip after-hours clubs: hobnobbing and scouting. Jimi would usually be requested to sit in, or whatever. In many ways, the requests were a part of the etiquette of polite English society. But Jimi and Chas began to take them up. Taking on a few select offers, the JHE played the exclusive Cromwellian

Club and the hip Bag O' Nails Club. There was no serious money involved, only the right kind of exposure. One night Jimi and company played the Scotch of St. James. Rod Harrod, the host, owed a great deal to Chas, who, as one of The Animals, had supported him when he left the Cromwellian because of a dispute with its owners.

The Scotch of St. James was located in a yard off of St. James Court. The ground floor had a bar and a restaurant, and the basement level was a dance floor surrounded by tables. The Beatles and the Stones had their own private tables, which were roped off and slightly elevated. It was not unusual for Princess Margaret and Lord Snowdon to show up. The decor was Scottish baronial, with plenty of sporrans, swords, and antlers. There was a couch on one side of the bandstand. Harrod had gone out of his way (discreetly, of course) to make sure that as many of the right people as possible were there. The basement was crowded with patrons, mainly standing on tiptoes to see the action. Jimi, Mitch and Noel played a superb set that featured Hey Joe. As soon as Kit Lambert, manager of The Who, and an activist in the new pop youth culture, heard it, he knew the song would be a hit and wasted no time in letting Chas know that he wanted the JHE to be on the new label he was launching, Track Records.

Chas and Kit went upstairs to discuss it further. Lambert was so enthusiastic over JHE that he was almost knocking over tables in his haste to sit down with Chas.

Chas was as enthusiastic about Track Records as Lambert was, but he tried to hide it. Track would not be launched until March. There was no doubt in Chas's mind that Hey Joe would be out before Christmas. But he told Lambert that he could promise the JHE to Track Records regardless of the deal made with another company, or whomever. Chas had been talking to record companies about the release of the JHE's first single. They were interested in more than a single, but since Chas was producing the master himself, with no upfront money on the record company's part, he really owed them nothing.

Soon Chas had the single in the can: Hey Joe, and Stone Free as the B-side. He took it to Decca, one of the companies he had been talking to. The A&R man there turned it down flatly, adding that he did not think Jimi had anything special. Panicked, Chas went directly back to Lambert, who reassured him of the validity of the recording, adding, as a vote of confidence, that he would take the record around to the record shops himself if necessary – but he doubted it would be. Reassured, Chas went off to Polydor Records with confidence. He secured a one-shot pressing and distribution deal, with further talks scheduled for the future.

Hey Joe was released on December 16, 1966, just before the Christmas holidays. It got radio air play at once, but there was really no way of telling how it would sell. The sound was strange and new, with supermusical effects hinting that something explosive would follow. Now the JHE had a product out on the market. Now was the time to begin to gig in earnest. On December 21, the JHE played Blaises Club – their lucky club. Although The Who were gigging at the Upper Cut, it was only a short distance from Blaises, and Peter Townshend showed up. Jeff Beck was there too, in the standing-room-only crowd.

The JHE got its first real write-up in Melody Maker in its "Caught in the Act" column. They talked of the star-packed crowd and the blown minds. They used words like "fantastic" and "exceptional" in describing Jimi's guitar playing, and also mentioning Jimi's playing with his teeth, Melody Maker forecasted him as "one of the big club names of 1967".

But Chas was edgy. It was difficult for him to enjoy the Christmas holiday. They were broke. The record was out. Now was the time to push through. He had to do something that would establish JHE in the New Year in London. Besides. they had no work lined up and there was no telling what would transpire in 1967. They were at a low ebb; they had to do something, and soon.

Chas decided to throw a party at the Bag O'Nails Club. Although it would ostensibly be a celebration, it would also be a showcase for Jimi. Chas invited all the promoters and tour bookers and the "in" people among whom they would be most comfortable. It was a gamble in which there was also a touch of desperation. Chas knew that if this push did not take hold, then it would be virtually the end of the Jimi Hendrix Experience. The only way for him to pay for their "reception" was to pawn five of his six guitars.

On the night of Chas's party, January 11, 1967, Hey Joe entered the charts. Although it was only Number 48, it was a very good sign. It was moving up fast. Now for the first time there was the possibility of Jimi being more than a passing curiosity or an interesting freak, but someone on the way up.

Chas chose the Bag O'Nails because it was right off Carnaby Street, the most fashionable street of the emergent "Flower Power" youth. Many rock stars were in attendance, seated at long tables facing the stage. It was evident they were "following" Jimi. A better following was impossible to buy. But there were numerous other novelties this crowd had followed and then tossed aside after a while. George Melly, the respected English cultural commentator, author, and jazz singer, has said, "Like great fish the top groups glide from club to club, and those whose pleasure is to follow in their wake swim with them."

Chas was looking for work, not in-crowd adulation. Philip Haywood, club owner and booker, invited the group to play as a support group to the New Animals at a series of out-of-London and in-London gigs for £25 a night. Chas was relieved. They would be able to eat.

The next night the JHE played second on the bill to the New Animals at one of Haywood's clubs, the 7½. Immediately it was obvious that it was impossible to bill Jimi as a second, or support act. There was no question who the press and rock stars had returned to see. The 7½, a new club just off Piccadilly, was delighted to have in the audience Mick Jagger, Marianne Faithfull, Peter Townshend, Anita Pallenberg, Eric Clapton, Linda Keith, and Glen Campbell.

Jimi played his standard set of songs: Hey Joe, Stone Free, Can You See Me?, Rock Me Baby, Like A Rolling Stone, Third

Stone From The Sun and Wild Thing. At this point it was a pleasure for them to be working for steady money with a breaking act on tour. It was like a dress rehearsal for their break, and the way Chas was gambling, they would break out as stars or not at all.

Jimi played the 7½ Club most of that week, with a one-day excursion to the Beachcomber Club in Nottingham on the fourteenth. On January 19 he played the Speakeasy. On the twenty-fifth, the Marquee Club. Things were beginning to snowball. He was playing the top clubs as if he were already an established artist.

At the Marquee, Kit Lambert asked Chas to allow him to bill the Jimi Hendrix Experience with The Who at Brian Epstein's Saville Theatre. Chas was delighted. The Saville was tops, and so were The Who. Finally Jimi was sharing the bill with a group of his calibre. It began to get around London that there would be a battle royal on January 29, 1967. A battle of the groups.

The Who vs. the Jimi Hendrix Experience concert, a tribute to Brian Epstein, was held on a Sunday. In attendance were Eric Clapton, Klaus Voorman, Linda Keith, John Lennon, Spencer Davis, Jack Bruce, Paul McCartney, and Lulu. Right from the announcement everyone knew it would be a famous concert. The two most outrageous groups in London duelling in feedback frenzy, full amps billowing forth decibels through theatre walls.

On February 4, Hey Joe came in Number 4 on the Melody Maker chart. That was it; Hey Joe was a hit. The February 5, 1967, gig at the Flamingo Club was like the premiere of the Jimi Hendrix Experience as a star attraction.

The Flamingo Club was notorious for its lackadaisical approach to the best of British rock. A hip room, the Flamingo catered to a steady clientele of beatnik-like insiders of the London underground. They were all too hip to the machinations of the British recording industry and its sundry promotion men. This club was the last in a long line of hip London clubs Hendrix and company had had to conquer and it was the toughest. The crowd at the Flamingo usually refrained from applauding in anything but the most token fashion.

Jimi opens at once with a jam meandering in heavy tempo. Then signalling in the blues with a long-distance call tremolo, he takes the band into Killing Floor. Straight-down boogie, up-tempo R&B chords – like an Apollo showtime theme truncated into an introduction to the Jimi Hendrix Experience. Then Jimi speaks from the wall of sound, "Thank you very much." The music ceases . . . "We'd like to continue on with a little tune, a very straight, ha, ha . . . Top 40 R&B rock'n'roll record. A little thing called Have Mercy, have mercy on me . . . BABY."

Noel Redding comes out with a Woolly Bully bass beat, Jimi chording blues rhythm licks and filling in the lead, they come to the bridge, the blues chord inverted theme that explains, as so often in R&B, with words and tune changes, the meaning of the plea.

Can You See Me?, Jimi's own tune, has the first really brilliant solo of the set spaced within an ample middle-bridge section that extends into the break where an elongated twang sustains for eight beats on the up-tempo, and then the ensemble returns to the back-beating wall of sound. Finally Jimi slows the pace, strumming soft chords against a simple run that sounds like a coffeehouse folk song.

"Right now, I'd like to try to do a song for you, a little thing by Bob Dylan called Like A Rolling Stone . . . I want to dedicate this song to a few people in this club."

It comes out more like a ballad with the guitar the dominant sound, picking out the melody.

Jimi's arrangement of Rock Me Baby is far from B.B. King's blues-style version. It is definitely super-tempo rock'n'roll all the way for the Experience.

Jimi slurs his announcement of the next number: "Thank you very much; and I'd like to try and do a little mixture of a whole lot of things in this one here . . . a little Muddy Waters version slightly." Jimi goes into the beginning of Muddy Waters's version of the traditional blues, Two Trains Running (which Muddy Waters called Still A Fool). From there he goes into a short solo circling about the few notes that compose the introductory phrases and extending them. And then just as easily slipping back into the original raunchy chords with short stroking chops to sing a couple of verses. And then straight and straight up into a psychedelic solo full of blue tonality yet not sounding like the blues at all. Then back to the verse, Jimi playing both the Muddy Waters lead and the Jimmie Rodgers second guitar of the original version at the same time.

> Well now there's two trains runnin'
> And neither one's going my way
> You know there's a one train runnin' at night
> The other one runs before day
> Runs before day, runs before day, runs before day...

Jimi plays with a little feedback at the end and then the song climaxes into pure distortion, which ends in an abrupt halt. The crowd comes alive for the first time. They cheer! Jimi answers with his Stratocaster whoozing a "thank you".

Jimi buzzes into Stone Free, the B-side of their record. The song builds slowly as he mumbles lyrics about being put down for his hair, for his clothes, and by his women, but he wants everyone to know – as the song builds to a screeching intensity – that he is STONE FREE. Without missing a beat the JHE segues right into their hit Hey Joe.

His solo is fantastic. His customized Fuzz Face full out creates endless peak distortions and sustains long lines that create their own vibrato from sheer force of volume. It is a thrilling sound that goes right through you. On the tag-out Jimi makes his guitar say "You better believe it, baby."

Wild Thing starts off with the fuzz hook that it was known for when The Troggs had it as their big hit. But Hendrix made Wild Thing a heavy, funky, mad metallic moan, full of the human sounds of the blues in primordial emotion. You *feel* Wild Thing. In the middle passage, he goes into a little bit of The Beatles' Day Tripper, contrasting the heavy sexual blues-laden drone of his Wild Thing with the flower-pop hit. Then he takes the song out. Rolling feedback in lava folds across an incredible terrain. Mitch Mitchell rolling, tramming, thunderous bombs against tingling cymbals that sound like a giant-ship emergency bell. Monster fucking sounds. Fire in pink noise. Thrashing in gargantuan moans, the overdriving amps blown full out reporting the oscillating feedback. Pulling back into a stellar void, the deep tonic of the bass becomes apparent as Jimi sets his guitar back into the drone note that began the song.

The Flamingo Club house MC picks up in the chaos: "Oh, let's hear it please for the Jimi Hendrix Experience . . ." But the great howl makes his shout a tiny voice. The audience has responded, but their applause and occasional cheers are overwhelmed by the protesting sound system. "OK, ladies and gentlemen. The three gentlemen you've seen on the stage have given you their very best. How about your very best for them? Would you gentlemen, everybody this time, put your hands together for THE JIMI HENDRIX EXPERIENCE . . ." The crowd erupts again in a very nice hand, with scattered cheers. An incredible hand for the Flamingo.

The MC continues, ". . . who were working out *so hard* that time. Thank you. I'm afraid that's all from those three gentlemen for the evening, but back on the stand later on goes The All-night Workers. Thank you very much for being so great and clapping so great for Jimi . . . Here we go for a few sounds, the one dedicated to Jimi, Please Don't Go."

A British cover of Baby, Please Don't Go screeches out from the speakers. It sweeps the club, penetrating to Jimi's dressing-room door, as the dressing room becomes more and more jammed with well-wishers and celebrities. Well, that was it. The Jimi Hendrix Experience is officially open for business – all offers and comers queued up.

Omnibus Press are the world's largest publishers of books about music and we have teamed up with the largest magazine about music to bring you the *Q/Omnibus Press Rock 'N' Roll Reader*.

Individual chapters have been chosen from a small selection of our catalogue and all books featured in the *Q/Omnibus Press Rock 'N' Roll Reader* can be purchased from the following bookshops in your area...

Scotland

Waterstones Booksellers
13-14 Princes Street, Edinburgh
031-556-3034

Waterstones Booksellers
132 Union Street, Glasgow
041-221-0890

Waterstones Booksellers
45-50 Princes Square, Glasgow
041-221-9650

Waterstones Booksellers
35 Commercial Street, Dundee
0382-200322

Waterstones Booksellers
144 Rose Street, South Lane,
Edinburgh
031-226-2666

Dillons The Bookstore
Argyle Street, Glasgow
041-248-4814

James Thin/Melven Book Shop
29 Union Street, Inverness
0463-233500

James Thin Booksellers
53-59 South Bridge, Edinburgh
031-556-6743

James Thin Booksellers
7-8 High Street, Dundee
0382-23999

James Thin Booksellers
18-26 Church Crescent, Dumfries
0387-54288

James Thin Booksellers
176 High Street, Perth
0738-35222

John Smith & Son
Byres Road, Glasgow
041-334-2769

John Smith & Son
57 St Vincent Street, Glasgow
041-221-7472

North of England

Waterstones Booksellers
9 Newton Mall, Cleveland Centre,
Middlesborough
0642-242682

Waterstones Booksellers
69 Saddler Street, Durham
091-383-1488

Waterstones Booksellers
93-97 Albion Street, Leeds
0532-444588

Waterstones Booksellers
24 Orchard Square, Sheffield
0742-728971

Dillons The Bookstore
Emerson Chambers, Blackett Street,
Newcastle upon Tyne
091-261-7757

Dillons The Bookstore
9-10 High Ousegate, York
0904-610044

Dillons The Bookstore
135-137 Briggate, Leeds
0532-470077

Dillons The Bookstore
27 Park Lane, Meadowhall Centre,
Sheffield
0742-568495

Dillons The Bookstore
1-3 The Cornmill Centre, Darlington
0325-363662

Our Price Limited
28 Blackett Bridge, Eldon Square,
Newcastle upon Tyne
091-261-2795

Athena Bookshop
16 The Parade, Metro Centre,
Gateshead
091-460-9794

Austicks City Bookshop
91 The Headrow, Leeds
0532-439607

Browns Books
22-28 George Street, Hull
0482-25413

Albert Gait Booksellers
Fountain Court, Freshney Place,
Grimsby
0472-342803

North West

Waterstones Booksellers
91 Deansgate, Manchester
061-832-1992

Waterstones Booksellers
17 St Anne's Square, Manchester
061-834-7055

Waterstones Booksellers
2-8 King Street, Lancaster
0524-61477

Waterstones Booksellers
3-5 Fishergate, Preston
0772-555766

Waterstones Booksellers
52 Bold Street, Liverpool
051-709-0866

Waterstones Booksellers
367 Lord Street, Southport
0704-501088

Dillons The Bookstore
12-16 Bold Street, Liverpool
051-708-6861

Dillons The Bookstore
2-4 St Anne's Square, Manchester
061-832-0424

Bramhall Bookshop
44 Bramhall Lane South, Bramhall
061-439-6002

Smiths Bookshop
41 Mesnes Street, Wigan
0942-42810

Bookland Music Shop,
12 Bridge Street Row, Chester
0244-347323

Alison's Bookshop
St Andrew's Court, Bolton
0204-384525

Midlands/East Midlands

Waterstones Booksellers
18-19 High Street, Shrewsbury
0743-248112

Waterstones Booksellers
1-5 Bridlesmith Gate, Nottingham
0602-484499

Waterstones Booksellers
24/26 High Street, Birmingham
021-633-4353

Waterstones Booksellers
18 The High Street,
Stratford upon Avon
0789-414418

Waterstones Booksellers
95 High Street, Worcester
0905-723397

Dillons The Bookstore
128 New Street, Birmingham
021-631-4333

Dillons The Bookstore
22 Cathedral Lanes Shopping Centre,
Broadgate, Coventry
0203-227151

Dillons The Bookstore
25 Wheelergate, Nottingham
0602-473531

Dillons The Bookstore
26 Market Street, Leicester
0533-545858

Dillons The Bookstore
Lewis Arcade, Potteries Shopping
Centre, Hanley, Stoke on Trent
0782-219550

Webberley Ltd
Percy Street, Hanley, Stoke on Trent
0782-268138

Wales/South West

Waterstones Booksellers
4-5 Milsom Street, Bath
0225-448515

Waterstones Booksellers
11a Union Gallery, The Galleries,
Broadmead, Bristol
0272-252274

Waterstones Booksellers
27 Regent Street, Swindon
0793-488838

Waterstones Booksellers
14-16 The Arcade, Bournemouth
0202-299449

Waterstones Booksellers
88/90 The Promenade, Cheltenham,
Gloucestershire
0242-512722

Dillons The Bookstore
1/2 St David's Link, The Hayes, Cardiff
0222-222723

Dillons The Bookstore
65-69 New George Street, Plymouth
0752-256699

Dillons The Bookstore
Roman Gate, 252 High Street, Exeter
0392-423044

Dillons The Bookstore
47-49 Union Street, Bristol
0272-299512

Ottakars Bookshop
15 Eastgate Street, Gloucester
0452-422464

South East

Waterstones Booksellers
35/39 North Street, Guildford, Surrey
0483-302919

Waterstones Booksellers
1063/7 Whitgift Centre,
Croydon, Surrey
081-686-7032

Waterstones Booksellers
20-22 Market Square, Bromley, Kent
081-464-6562

Waterstones Booksellers
120 Terminus Road,
Eastbourne, East Sussex
0323-735676

Dillons The Bookstore
Unit S9, The Bentall Centre,
Kingston upon Thames, Surrey
081-974-6811

Sherratt & Hughes
75 The Mall, Broadway Shopping
Centre, Bexley, Kent
081-301-4411

Sherratt & Hughes
94 Above Bar, Southampton, Hants
0703-639414

Read All About It
69 East Street, Brighton, Sussex
0273-205824

Albion Bookshop
29 Albion Street, Broadstairs, Kent
0843-862876

East Anglia
Selected range available from:

Athena Gallery
30 Liberty II Shopping Centre,
Mercury Gardens, Romford
0708-751767

Dillons The Bookstore
310 Lakeside Shopping Centre,
West Thurrock, Essex
0708-890363

Dillons The Bookstore
12-13 High Street, Colchester, Essex
0206-561307

Athena Gallery
30 Lakeside Shopping Centre,
West Thurrock, Essex
0708-890211

Waterstones Booksellers
The Old Library, 16 Culver Precinct,
Colchester, Essex
0206-767623

Dillons The Bookstore
22 Sidney Street, Cambridge
0223-351688

Athena Gallery
19 Lion Yard, Cambridge
0223-69890

Waterstones Booksellers
6-7 Bridge Street, Cambridge
0223-300123

Heffers
20 Trinity Street, Cambridge
0223-358351

Hatchards
Buttermarket Street, Ipswich
0473-257761

Athena Gallery
5 Lower Mall, Tower Ramparts,
Ipswich
0473-230416

Athena Gallery
7 Rampant Horse Street, Norwich
0603-628867

Jarrold & Sons Limited
London Street, Norwich
0603-660661

London & Home Counties

Waterstones Booksellers
12 Wimbledon Bridge, Wimbledon,
London SW19
081-543-9899

Dillons The Bookstore
19/23 Oxford Street, London W1
071-434-9759

Dillons The Bookstore
Units 7/8 The Galleria, Comet Way,
Hatfield
0707-270161

Dillons The Bookstore
48/52 Kensington High Street,
London W8
071-938-2228

Dillons The Bookstore
82 Gower Street, London WC1
071-636-1577

Dillons The Bookstore
Charter Place, 69 High Street,
Watford, Herts
0923-240356

Dillons The Bookstore
220-226 Chiswick High Road,
London W4
081-995-3559

Dillons The Bookstore
Units 31-33, Friars Square,
Aylesbury, Bucks
0296-23153

Dillons The Bookstore
William Baker House,
Broad Street, Oxford
0865-790212

Dillons The Bookstore
Units B&C, The Grand Buildings,
Trafalgar Square, London WC2
071-839-4411

The Carnaby Street General Store,
5/7 Carnaby Street, London W1
071-437-6824

Athena Bookshop
Trocadero Centre, Coventry Street,
London W1
071-734-5061

Athena Bookshop
1/4 Leicester Square, London WC2
071-437-6780

Athena Gallery
Unit 6a, Crown Walk Arcade,
Milton Keynes, Bucks
0908-670086

Books Etc
66 Victoria Street, London SW1
071-931-0677

Books Etc
16 Whiteleys of Bayswater,
London W2
071-229-3865

Books Etc
120 Charing Cross Road, London W1
071-379-6838

Rock Circus
The London Pavilion,
1 Piccadilly Circus, London W1
071-734-7203

Ottakars Bookshop
16 High Street, Banbury, Oxon
0295-270498

Book Castle
12 Church Street, Dunstable, Beds
0582-605670

Blackwells Music Shop
38 Holywell Street, Oxford
0865-792792

Pemberton Booksellers
18 Mill Street, Bedford
0234-364740

Friar Street Bookshop
142-143 Friar Street, Reading, Berks
0734-573082

Ireland

Selected range available from:

Eason, 40-42 Lower O'Connell Street,
Dublin
01-873-3811

Eason, 29 Main Street, Bangor,
Co Down
0247-472042

Eason, 111/112 Patrick Street, Cork
021-270477

Eason, 9 O'Connell Street, Limerick
061-419588

Eason, 33 Shop Street, Galway
091-62284

Eason, 16 Ann Street, Belfast
0232-328566

Eason, 34 Bow Street, Lisburn
0846-670561

Eason, 2/3 Buttercrane Centre, Newry
0693-61037

Great rock reads

Now that your fancy has been well and truly tickled, how best can you get your sticky mitts on these mind-blowing books, and hundreds more besides? Hard cash, moolah, spondulicks, in short, some of your hard-earned coin of the realm. But wait, save the shoe leather, leave the car at home, throw another log on the fire, sit back, relax, and let the books come to you.

Direct to your door

Every book featured in the *Q/Omnibus Rock 'N' Roll Reader* is available direct to your fireside chair. If you think we're a book club, we're not. You *never* have to buy another book from us.

Free postage & packing

What's more, we don't charge the equivalent of the Brazilian National Debt in postage & packing... in fact, for readers of Q who order using our nifty reply-paid card, we'll charge you absolutely nothing, nix, de nada.
The price you see is the price you pay.

Money back guarantee

And once you've paid that price, every book carries our no quibble, money back guarantee. If you are not completely satisfied, return the book to us in saleable condition within 7 days, and we'll refund every red cent. Seems fairly quibble-free to me.

The last bit

Okay, let's go over it again. You can order using our FREEPOST reply card, you don't pay a bean for postage & packing, you never have to buy another book from us, and to cap it all, you can relax secure in the knowledge that you'll get every penny back, unless completely satisfied. Simply fill in the card, sit back, and contemplate the prompt arrival of Her Majesty's Postal Service. Seems like now would be a very good time to do just that.

Choose from 200 rather good books

Run the Rock 'n' Pop gamut from the proverbial A-Z...

AC/DC : Hell Ain't No Bad Place To Be £9.95
AC/DC : HM Photo Book £9.95
AC/DC : Illustrated Biography £9.95
ADAMS, Bryan : Illustrated Biography £5.95
AEROSMITH : The Fall & Rise Of £9.95
BARRETT, Syd : Crazy Diamond £9.95
BEATLES : Complete Lyrics £9.95
BEATLES : In Their Own Words £7.95
BEATLES : In Their Own Words (After The Break Up) £7.95
BEATLES : With The £7.95
BLACK CROWES, The £7.95
BOLAN, Marc : Electric Warrior £7.95
BUSH, Kate : Secret History £7.95
BUSH, Kate : Visual Documentary £9.95
CAGE, John : Conversing With £9.95
CHER : In Her Own Words £7.95
CHER : Visual Documentary £12.95
CLAPTON, Eric : In His Own Words £7.95
CLASH, The : The New Visual Documentary £9.95
COCKER, Joe : With A Little Help... £7.95
COHEN, Leonard : Prophet Of The Heart £12.95
CRAMPS, The : The Wild Wild World Of £8.95
CURE, The £4.95
CURE, The : Songwords £9.95
CURE, The : Ten Imaginary Years £12.95
CURE, The : Visual Documentary £12.95
DEAN, James : In His Own Words £7.95
DEATH OF RHYTHM & BLUES £6.95
DOORS, The : Illustrated History £14.95
DOORS, The : In Their Own Words £7.95
DOORS, The : Lyrics 1965 - 71 £7.95

DYLAN, Bob : In His Own Words £7.95
DYLAN, Bob : Performing Artist Vol 1 1960 - 1973 £9.95
DYLAN, Bob : Performing Artist Vol 2 1974 - 1986 £9.95
FAITHFULL, Marianne : As Tears Go By £7.95
GOTHIC ROCK BLACK BOOK £8.95
GUNS N' ROSES : In Their Own Words £7.95
GUNS N' ROSES : Live ! £4.95
GUNS N' ROSES : Lowlife £8.95
GUNS N' ROSES : Over The Top £12.95
HENDRIX, Jimi : A Biography £8.95
HENDRIX, Jimi : 'Scuse Me... £9.95
HENDRIX, Jimi : Visual Documentary £12.95
IRON MAIDEN : What Are We Doing This For? £9.95
JACKSON, Michael : In His Own Words £7.95
JACKSON, Michael : Live & Dangerous £4.95
JOHN, Elton : In His Own Words £7.95
JOHN, Elton : Visual Documentary £12.95
JOY DIVISION : An Ideal For Living £7.95
k.d. lang : Illustrated Biography £5.95
LED ZEPPELIN : A Celebration £12.95
LED ZEPPELIN : In Their Own Words £7.95
LED ZEPPELIN : Visual Documentary £8.95
LENNON, John : Art & Music £7.95
LENNON, John : In His Own Words £7.95
MADONNA (Cahill) £12.95
MADONNA : In Her Own Words £7.95
MADONNA : New Illustrated Biography £9.95
MADONNA : Scrapbook £12.95
MADONNA : Stylebook £9.95
MARLEY, Bob : Catch A Fire £9.95
MARLEY, Bob : In His Own Words £7.95

McCARTNEY, Paul : In His Own Words £7.95

METALLICA : Visual Documentary £9.95

MISSION, The : Names Are For Tombstones Baby £6.99

MONROE, Marilyn : In Her Own Words £7.95

MORRISON, Jim : Feast of Friends £12.95

MORRISON, Jim : Lords & New Creatures £5.95

MORRISON, Jim : The End £4.95

MORRISSEY : In His Own Words £7.95

MORRISSEY & MARR : Severed Alliance £9.95

MYSTERY TRAIN £12.95

NEW ORDER & JOY DIVISION : Pleasures... £6.95

NIRVANA £4.95

NIRVANA : & The Sound of Seattle £12.95

OTWAY, John : Cor Baby... £4.95

PARSONS, Gram : Hickory Wind £12.95

PEARL JAM : Illustrated Biography £4.95

PINK FLOYD : Visual Documentary £12.95

PRESLEY, Elvis £12.95

PRESLEY, Elvis : In His Own Words £7.95

PRESLEY, Elvis : The Final Years £7.95

PRINCE : A Documentary £12.95

PRINCE : Illustrated Biography £9.95

QUEEN : In Their Own Words £7.95

QUEEN : New Visual Documentary £12.95

REED, Lou : Growing Up In Public £7.95

REED, Lou : & The Velvet Underground £7.95

R.E.M. : Remarks £8.95

ROCK FAMILY TREES £14.95

ROCK LIVES £16.95

ROLLING STONES : In Their Own Words £7.95

RUSH : Visions £8.95

SEX & DRUGS & ROCK & ROLL £12.95

SEX PISTOL : I Was A Teenage £7.95

SEX PISTOLS : Chaos £9.95

SEX PISTOLS : Day By Day £7.95

SEX PISTOLS : File £7.95

SEX PISTOLS : Never Mind The B*ll*cks £7.95

SEX PISTOLS : The Inside Story £7.95

SIMPLY RED : Illustrated Biography £12.95

SIOUXSIE & THE BANSHEES : Photo Book £7.95

SMITHS : The Complete Story £7.95

SMITHS : Visual Documentary £14.95

SPRINGSTEEN, Bruce : In His Own Words £7.95

SPRINGSTEEN, Bruce : No Surrender £6.95

STEWART, Rod : Visual Documentary £9.95

STING : In His Own Words £7.95

SUEDE : Illustrated Biography £4.95

VELVET UNDERGROUND : Beyond £6.95

VELVET UNDERGROUND : Uptight £7.95

VICIOUS, Sid : Sid's Way £9.95

WRITTEN IN MY SOUL £12.95

XTC : Chalkhills & Children £9.95

YOUNG, Neil : Don't Be Denied £9.95

ZAPPA, Frank : In His Own Words £7.95

ZAPPA, Frank : Visual Documentary £12.95

This is but a small vignette of our full list. Use the enclosed Freepost reply card to obtain your very own complimentary catalogue.

All prices correct at time of going to press.